Xenophon Press Library

Xenophon Press continues to bring new works to print in the English language whether they be new works, such as this, or translations of older works. Xenophon Press is dedicated to the preservation of classical equestrian literature. Here is a sampling of the current offering from Xenophon Press available at

www.XenophonPress.com

30 Years with Master Nuno Oliveira, Michel Henriquet 2011

A Rider's Survival from Tyranny, Charles de Kunffy 2012

Another Horsemanship, Jean-Claude Racinet, 1994

Art of the Lusitano, Yglesias de Oliveira, 2012

Baucher and His School, General Decarpentry 2011

Dressage in the French Tradition, Dom Diogo de Bragança 2011

École de Cavalerie Part II, François Robichon de la Guérinière 1992

François Baucher: The Man and His Method, Baucher and Nelson, 2013

Gymnastic Exercises for Horses Volume II, Eleanor Russell 2013

Healing Hands, Dominique Giniaux, DVM 1998

Legacy of Master Nuno Oliveira, Stephanie Millham 2013

Methodical Dressage of the Riding Horse..., Faverot de Kerbrech 2010

Racinet Explains Baucher, Jean-Claude Racinet 1997

The Art and Science of Riding in Lightness, Stodulka 2014

The Art of Traditional Dressage, Volume I DVD, de Kunffy 2013

The Écuyères of the Nineteenth Century in the Circus, Hilda Nelson 2001

The Ethics and Passions of Dressage Expanded Edition, de Kunffy 203

The Gymnasium of the Horse, Gustav Steinbrecht 2011

The Italian Tradition of Equestrian Art, Tomassini 2014

The Maneige Royal, Antoine de Pluvinel 2010

The Portuguese School of Equestrian Art, de Oliveira and da Costa, 2012

The Spanish Riding School & Piaffe and Passage, Decarpentry 2013

Total Horsemanship, Jean-Claude Racinet 1999

Wisdom of Master Nuno Oliveira, Antoine de Coux 2012

Dominique Giniaux, D.V.M.
"The Horse Listener"

Equine Osteopathy:
"WHAT THE HORSES HAVE TOLD ME"

The Expanded Edition

Translated by Jean-Claude Racinet,
Richard F. Williams and Danielle Goulding

© Xenophon Press 1996
© Xenophon Press 2014

Translated by Jean-Claude Racinet, Richard Williams and Danielle Goulding.

Edited by Richard Williams and Frances Williams M.D.

All rights reserved. No part of this work may be reproduced or transmitted in any form or by any means, electronic or mechanical, including photocopying, or by any information storage or retrieval system except by a written permission from the publisher.

Published by Xenophon Press LLC

7518 Bayside Road, Franktown, Virginia 23354-2106, U.S.A.

XenophonPress@gmail.com

Equine Osteopathy: What the Horses Have Told Me

eBook ISBN: 9780933316485

Print edition

ISBN-10   0933316445

ISBN-13   9780933316447

Cover design by Naia Poyer

Original French edition © 1992 by Editions Lamarre, Paris

Copyright © 1996 by Xenophon Press

Copyright © 2014 by Xenophon Press LLC

Illustrations by author and Natalya Romanovskaya

Cover photo by Suzanne Lammi

Previous Print edition: *What the Horses Have Told Me* (1992)

ISBN-10: 0933316070

ISBN-13: 9780933316072

TABLE OF CONTENTS

Introduction to the Expanded Edition	7
Preface	9
Foreword	11
Translator's foreword	13
Part One: Osteopathy as Seen From the Horse	15
Chapter 1: Basic notions	17
Chapter 2: The various techniques	23
Chapter 3: Structural manipulations	27
Chapter 4: Personal hypotheses on the mode of action	33
The individual confronted with the manipulations	33
The circuits of action of the manipulations	37
Chapter 5: Life	43
Part Two: The Horse Seen From an Osteopathic Point of View	49
Chapter 6: The vertebra-organ link	51
Chapter 7: The sacrum	53
Chapter 8: The lumbar vertebrae	57
Chapter 9: The thoracic vertebrae	61
Chapter 10: The cervical vertebrae	65
Chapter 11: Recapitulatory Chart	69
Chapter 12: Balance of the hind legs	71
Chapter 13: Balance of the front legs	77
Chapter 14: The saddle	83
Chapter 15: Working *downwards*, bending	87
Chapter 16: Correct Collection & elevation of the head and neck	95
Chapter 17: What to do when facing a problem	103
Chapter 18: The manipulations	107
Conclusion	109
Appendix 1: *Dura Lex, Sed Lex* **by Jean-Claude Racinet**	111
Epilogue: Twenty years of dialogue with horses	119
About the Author & About this Book	131

Introduction to the Expanded Edition

Twenty-four years have passed, since Dr. Giniaux's book first appeared in print in French. Four years later, in 1996 the first English edition was published by Xenophon Press. Subsequently, Dr. Giniaux expanded his writing in the German edition and the French re-edition.

Demand for Dr. Giniaux's ground breaking work in equine osteopathy continues. Xenophon Press has expanded this volume from the first publication to include updated material from all of the language editions. The new, Recapitulatory Chart in Chapter 11 has been updated to include all of Dr. Giniaux's dicoveries. This volume includes the *Appendix I: Dura Lex, Sed Lex* not included in either of the French or German editions. *The Epilogue: 20 Years later* has never been published in English until now; this is thanks to the translation efforts of Danielle Goulding. This 'expanded edition' is the most complete release of Dr. Ginaux's work by this title.

We thank Benedictine Giniaux for encouraging Xenophon Press to make Dr. Giniaux's work available to all of those interested. A huge debt of gratitude is owed to Frances A. Williams M.D. for her excellent editing specifically bringing medical accuracy to the terminology and added clarity of meaning to the prose. Further acknowledgement goes to Stephanie Millham for her excellent copy editing and exactitude.

We hope you find this complete edition relevant in addressing major and minor alterations in your horse's locomotion and his physiology.

—Richard F. Williams
Editor-in-Chief
Publisher
Xenophon Press LLC.

Preface

The key of this book lies in its title: *What the horses have told me.* It opens the door to understanding the mechanism of osteopathy.

As his writings unfold, Dominique Giniaux shares with us his reflections and invites us to participate in his experiences with the equine world.

His vast knowledge of horses, his insatiable curiosity of the phenomena of nature and creatures, his immense common sense, and his indisputable creative skills led him to become the veterinarian practitioner whom the greatest among the European horse world have chosen to "fix" the most famous stars of the show grounds and the race tracks.

Once, he came to my office with the wide, astonished look which was familiar to him, and told me:

"Please, teach me osteopathy."

Attentive, skillful, and precise, he rapidly became a master in the art of sensing and understanding the subtle mechanisms of our human machinery.

His creative skill and his knack for transposing have allowed him to give the horse that which I, for so many years, have tried to give the human. His work is genuine; he is the only one in Europe and perhaps in the world who treats horses according to the principles and techniques of modern osteopathy.

In spite of his classical upbringing in veterinary medicine, he grasped with astonishing rapidity the elements which make, out of osteopathy, in its concepts as well as in its practice a treatment system totally different from allopathic medicine.

He knows perfectly well, as any qualified osteopath does, that symptoms are mere walk-ons [supernumeraries] on the stage where the drama of our organism's life is played; walk-ons [supernumeraries] whose names do not feature on the cast of the osteopathic check-up. The true actors are the functional troubles which initiate the disruption of our precious equilibrium.

He knows that to coordinate these troubles amounts to putting together the pathologic puzzle piece by piece, while objectively listening to the patient, human or equine, in order to build the therapeutic web which will restore vigor and harmony to this patient's daily life.

Written for the lay public, this book comes as true information on the existence of an alternative way to experience and conceive medicine, whether animal or human.

It is a real testimony of a distinctive quality of the relationship between practitioner and patient, and its authenticity is not its lesser merit.

Jean Josse
Osteopath DO, MRO
Former Pedagogic Director of the Sutherland
College of Osteopathic Medicine,
Co-founder of the Federation of Osteopaths of France.

Foreword

The first concern of any kind of medicine is to listen to the patient and know the questions to ask in order to determine accurately which troubles that the patient is experiencing.

In classical veterinary medicine, dialogue is unfortunately indirect; questions and answers are sometimes altered by the intermediaries. People in charge of the animal may misinterpret its behavior. Furthermore the proceedings meant for helping the diagnosis are not always reliable. Radiography, for one, is not always reliable because a lame horse may present a bony deformation visible on an x-ray film and it may be that this very lesion is not what he is suffering from!

I practiced this allopathic medicine while trying, as all my colleagues do, to limit the risks of error resulting from the intermediaries and the problems of "communication" between the animal and the practitioner.

Whereupon I discovered human osteopathy[1] which taught me how to ask questions directly to the body of the patient without any other means but my hands. I found out that while the individual may be mistaken when trying to describe his distinctive troubles, his body never lies and shouts out perfectly palpable evidence.

Armed with this direct language, this "body embrace," I have been questioning sick horses every day for five years now.

---

1 [Editor's note: Andrew Taylor Still defined osteopathy as: "that science which consists of such exact, exhaustive, and verifiable knowledge of the structure and function of the human mechanism, anatomical, physiological and psychological, including the chemistry and physics of its known elements, as has made discoverable certain organic laws and remedial resources, within the body itself, by which nature under the scientific treatment peculiar to osteopathic practice, apart from all ordinary methods of extraneous, artificial, or medicinal stimulation, and in harmonious accord with its own mechanical principles, molecular activities, and metabolic processes, may recover from displacements, disorganizations, derangements, and consequent disease, and regained its normal equilibrium of form and function in health and strength."

I ask them questions with my mere hands, and it is through them that they answer me. I also treat them with my hands, and the results are encouraging.

In the course of this ongoing dialogue, the horses have enlightened me on the "*modus operandi*" and the value of osteopathy. Thus, what I am discovering daily gets more precise as it unveils increasingly vast horizons on this means of considering pathology.

I am far from having investigated the entire subject, and what I have summed up in the first part of this book is only a step toward a completely new and often amazing field of knowledge.

The little I might have acquired and verified on occasion through these exchanges has allowed me to already set forth a few rules of behavior when facing a horse, and I explain in part two of this book the general rules of conduct which proceed from it.

Therefore, after having seen what the horses have brought to the understanding of osteopathy, we will see what osteopathy can already bring to the horses.

For instance, some unsafe movements may beget chronic troubles which have apparently nothing to do with locomotive problems. Osteopathy explains this very well and hence allows us to determine which movements are dangerous and to know what should never be done with the skeleton of a horse. From this discovery stems a few very simple rules of behavior for locomotive problems of the working horse. We shall see, moreover, that the rules of horsemanship have not been set forth randomly, for they are the result of long experience.

Since there are no existing written documents about equine osteopathy, I could only progress through a daily "manual listening" and this book collects all that the horses have told me to date....

Dominique Giniaux D.V. M.

Translator's foreword

Eleven years ago, our mutual publisher and friend Jean-Louis Gouraud sent me Dr. Giniaux's manuscript of *Les chevaux m'ont dit* for reading and commenting.

I must acknowledge that, at the time, I had completely overlooked the importance of Dr. Giniaux's work from the trainer's point of view, all the more since I felt ill at ease with some of the riding procedures of Dr. Giniaux.

At that time, things were "simple." There were two distinct realms: the realm of the veterinarian, who deals with sick horses, and the realm of the trainer, who deals with sometimes (often, as it happens) stiff and poorly balanced, but at least sound horses. Therefore, all of the osteopathic information provided by Dr. Giniaux was for me only a matter of "general culture," certainly interesting in itself, but whose practical application would probably be scarce.

Four years went by.

Then *Spirit* came about. *Spirit* was—and still is—a cantankerous gray Thoroughbred mare who, after two years of training—and training by me, would you believe it?—was still fighting like hell at the canter. So I decided that *Spirit* was probably having a physical problem. This was a victory over myself, since I was so proud and so vain that I tended to consider any admittance by the rider of a physical problem with the horse (unless the horse was dead lame) as a cop out.

Looking at her in her stall, I noticed that she was urinating poorly. "Great!" I thought, "she has a kidney problem, and that's why she can't canter; she's in pain." But all the tests came back negative. No kidney problem.

I set out then to do what Dr. Giniaux described in this book, and tried to palpate *Spirit's* back. And lo and behold, what I found was that the last vertebra, next to the pelvis, was noticeably offset to the left. I called Dr. Giniaux at once. He told me that it was the sixth lumbar, that my observation on *Spirit's* poor urination was pertinent, since a lesion with the sixth lumbar brings about these difficulties. And he described to me the manipulation I had to perform.

This would be the beginning of my trek toward the light.

Now, every time an apparently unsolvable riding problem would surface with my horses or my students', instead of casting the blame on the horse's "stubbornness" or the rider's lack of skill, I would take off the saddle and systematically palpate, and then call Dr. Giniaux. I rapidly learned a lot in this way and gave a lot of money to the phone company, but believe me, this was a good investment!

Dr. Giniaux says in this book that he can't give away the details of the manipulations, because of the possible misuse that would result from it. I am greatly honored that he made an exception with me.

Seven years have gone by, but I am still harrowing Dr. Giniaux with the most unexpected questions, and jeopardizing my personal finances as I am in the process of becoming the best client of "you guessed it," my phone company. These conversations with Dr. Giniaux have brought me much knowledge. But I pride myself that I have partially paid my debt to Dr. Giniaux, since I drew his attention to some aspects of horsemanship, for instance the knowledge of the Baucherist "flexion of the jaw," which he has introduced in his osteopathic manipulations.

For this reason, and since after eleven years (this book dates back to 1985) Dr. Giniaux has broadened the field of his observations and "tuned up" his osteopathic procedures. It was tempting to modify accordingly this English version of *"Les Chevaux m'ont dit."* Yet I decided not to do so, in order to present an authentic translation of the book as it was written.

However, Dr. Giniaux agreed on three things: First, this foreword, albeit lengthy. Second, a few footnotes by your servant. Third, a copy of an article published in *DRESSAGE & CT #112* (January 1996) as an appendix.

Jean-Claude Racinet

Part One: Osteopathy As Seen From The Horse

Chapter 1

Basic notions

The first problem posed by osteopathy is one of etymology: "osteopathy[2]" means bone disease, and therefore does not have anything to do with what we intend to speak of. The term has been retained out of fidelity to the memory of its founder who wanted to express that he was treating the body through the skeleton.

Other terms have been brought forth, like "osteotherapy," or "structural re-equilibration," but none were satisfying and the habit has been kept by tradition.

A slightly different school took the name of "etiopathy" in order to differentiate itself, but the term is not better fitting ("disease of the causes"). Etiopaths work practically in the same spirit as osteopaths; they made a point to distance themselves from osteopaths, out of an attempt to oppose some excesses and foster more rigor in the reasonings. These laudable scruples have sometimes the disadvantage of limiting the possibilities. But it is about mere nuances which allow the two schools to criticize each other cordially while being as competent as the other!

As I am myself in total agreement with the theoretical basis set forth by the one who chose the word osteopathy, I shall retain this term, which, over time, has acquired a precise significance.

Osteopathy is not a method of treatment; it is a way to conceive of a living organism in its wholeness. Therefore, it is to be classified with "holistic" medicines, as for instance acupuncture, which never deals with only one organ, or only one trouble of the patient. Let's not forget that "individual" means "that cannot be broken down into several pieces."

---

2   [Editor's Note: Alternate definition from the Greek *osto*:bone, *pathos*:feeling.]

For the record, I find it amusing that classical western medicine never speaks of "individual," as it chose the term "patients" to designate its clients.

It is improper to say that an individual was treated by means of osteopathy; one should say that he/she was treated by an osteopath, or thanks to osteopathy.

Osteopathy is not a set of manipulations, it is a particular approach to the equilibrium of a living organism and its pathology; it resorts to diverse types of manipulations in order to reach its goals.

With the exception of the field of cranial manipulations, osteopaths have not invented any manipulation; the manual techniques they are using in order to meet their purpose were known the world over since the most remote antiquity.

Physicians or veterinarians who criticize these practices probably ignore what Hippocrates wrote, a few pages away from the famed oath they all have taken: "...I hold in high esteem the practitioners of manual medicine..." In all ancient civilizations, one finds references to manual therapists in order to treat some troubles with individuals. Chinese acupuncture is one of them, and there have always been "bone setters" everywhere.

Only during the twentieth century did physicians begin pretending they have invented the manipulations so as to monopolize them for the sake of their own trade. They perhaps codified them in some cases, but they did not invent anything.

The origins of osteopathy lie in its way of conceiving health, and this resulted in the utilization of diverse, already known manipulations.

The basic concept of osteopathy was discovered in the nineteenth century by Andrew Taylor Still[3], an American physician.

This first osteopath, A.T. Still, enunciated the two following statements:

"Structure governs function."

---

3   [Editor's Note: (August 6, 1828 – December 12, 1917) was the founder of osteopathy and osteopathic medicine. He was also a physician and surgeon, author, inventor and Kansas territorial and state legislator. He was one of the founders of Baker University, the oldest four-year college in the state of Kansas, and was the founder of the American School of Osteopathy (now A.T. Still University), the world's first osteopathic medical school, in Kirksville, Missouri.]

Which means that a living organism cannot function normally if its supporting structures have lost part of their mobility.

"The rule of the artery is sovereign."

If blood circulation is impaired, the affected organ is weakened, and does not fulfil its function correctly, or becomes rapidly susceptible to infection; it cannot fight the nesting of a bacteria or a virus which takes advantage of its weakness.

These two sentences encompass the whole of osteopathy; if, in some place in the body, a bone, a muscle, a tendon, or a ligament cannot play its part freely because it is blocked by a spasm, blood circulation is impaired, resulting in troubles in the area which the affected vessels should irrigate.

When we understand this concept, we can do all that's possible to preserve or restore the mobility of all the structural elements. These comprise the skeleton and its main parts, the spinal column, but also include all the tendons, ligaments, and muscles which interrelate in the structure to assure the movements necessary for life. The smallest ligament linking one organ to the whole must be free so as not to impair any function.

The spinal column is of great importance because it constitutes the main beam of the body, and through its multiple joints, allows the performance of very complex movements; but it is also because it hosts the spinal cord which is the "distribution cable" of the entire nervous system. All the nervous fibers stemming from it must meander their way through the vertebral joints.

Before even speaking of manipulation, to be an osteopath consists of knowing how to palpate an individual and thus detect all the elements of its organism which have lost their natural mobility. This requires a strenuous training which little by little leads one to an incredible finesse of palpation. The smallest tensions detected at the level of the skin give a bounty of information on the state of the body's deepest organs.

For instance, with a horse suffering from colic, the more or less impaired mobility of the skin of the abdomen informs the practitioner about the state of each affected organ. The osteopaths speak of "manual listening" to give an idea of the improved perception they achieve. This expression is all the more fitting as their hands sense the minute vibrations of the body, whether they result from muscular spasms or the circulation of energy as explained by the Chinese system of acupuncture.

Some laugh at the mentioning of such a refined palpation, but touch is a sense which can be refreshed and thence become very rich. Just try to decode a text written in Braille, bearing in mind that the blind do it at the very same speed as you read; you will realize that the sense of touch in most individuals is very undeveloped to start with. We content ourselves with so little since the usual requirements of daily life do not necessitate more. One has to admit that some can train themselves and reach a degree of perception hardly imaginable.

The osteopaths particularly stress the palpation of the spinal column, because most organic or peripheral problems are accompanied with a vertebral blocking at the level where the related nerves stem from the spinal cord. One will rarely find a peripheral trouble which is not accompanied by a vertebral osteopathic lesion. By starting the check-up with the spinal column, the osteopath detects lesions which reveal other possible troubles. One can therefore draw a chart of the organs and functions thus connected to each level of the spinal column; we shall produce later on this list which helps in understanding the internal pathology of horses affected with some locomotive problems.

Before going any further, I want to stress a detail I consider important:

The famed difference between veterinarians (or allopathic physicians) and osteopaths is about a bogus problem which is not close to being solved, because the two sides don't speak the same language.

Some veterinarians—very competent ones in their specialty—affirm, orally and even in writing, that a horse's vertebrae are never displaced, and that it just takes looking at a horse's skeleton to realize that it is impossible to manipulate them.

They are right if they mean that the vertebrae of a horse are never dislocated, and therefore do not need to be realigned.

To humor those persons and show them that you understand, make a point of not saying that your horse has a displaced vertebra, but that he has a vertebra which does not move anymore, a blocked vertebra.

There are no such things as displaced vertebrae to be reset, but rather blocked vertebrae to be freed.

This important detail having been dealt with, it is no longer nonsensical to imagine that vertebral manipulations are possible, even with such a big animal as a horse.

Here comes the second part of the osteopath's work: upon having palpated and diagnosed the lesions, he uses his hands to give back to the body the mobility it has lost.

It is obvious that he/she who would learn the techniques of manipulation without setting out to learn how to palpate could not call him/herself an osteopath. He/she would be inefficient and even dangerous sometimes for his/her patients.

Altogether, the risk is twofold; a contrary manipulation could entail more or less serious troubles for the animal, but it also may be dangerous for him/her who practices it, since it generally triggers off a violent reaction from the horse.

The horse indeed, like all the other animals, lends himself rather readily to the manipulation, provided it be perfectly indicated and perfectly performed.

For the reasons I just brought forth, I shall give in this book few details on the techniques of manipulation of a horse. I shall, instead, give a few main features and provide the reasoning which allows one to understand why such a technique in possible.

Therefore, I will first demonstrate that it is not unrealistic to envision manual therapies on such big animals, and I will show that the basic pattern of manipulation also applies to horsemanship. If well understood, this simple reasoning gives any rider directions to follow when a horse presents locomotive problems.

Next, I will outline what happens at the level of a vertebral blocking, and what principle allows one to unlock it easily. But let us first speak about the differences in theory which may appear from one osteopath to another.

Chapter 2

The various techniques

I do not pretend to have perfected equine osteopathy and I admit freely that another osteopath may use other means which suit him better. I started alone, with human techniques learned from Jean Josse. Thus, I had to imagine proceedings suitable for the result I was looking for.

Actually, one can observe some differences between osteopaths, but they are merely technical. The principles and goals are always the same: evaluate the losses of mobility related to the troubles suffered by an individual and treat them manually. The decision as to which manipulation to choose depends on the lesion and the practitioner, each favoring the manipulation which he/she "feels" best.

At the two extremes of the spectrum, there exist two apparently different forms of osteopathy:

• Structural osteopathy, which is definitely mechanistic; it consists of resolving manually all the mechanical obstacles to the blocked circulation, whether joint or ligament blockings. The ligaments considered may be those which support the *viscera* in the abdominal cavity. From this point of view, osteopathy makes it a principle to allow the free circulation of the liquids in charge of the nutrition and drainage of the ensemble (blood, lymphatics, etc.).

The starting point of this endeavor is the spinal column, since it is the support of the nervous system, which controls the circulation, autonomic equilibrium, and various hormones, i.e., all which Chinese acupuncture gathers under the heading of "Energy."

Fluidic osteopathy works directly on the fluids whose circulation may be hampered in some places. It reinforces their currents and controls their course so as to make the flux itself sweep off the obstacles it encounters.

The osteopaths who have opted for this latter tendency work therefore directly on the Energy, which itself liberates its own trajectories. This way to approach osteopathy was born from the discovery of a student of Andrew Taylor Still, W.G. Sutherland, who noticed that the bones of the skull are not welded, but articulated, and that these joints work like hinges. He found out that every skull bloats and unbloats rhythmically (which is perfectly palpable with some training) and he got the streak of genius to understand that this movement is linked to the variations of pressure of the cerebrospinal liquid. This liquid is held in a canal which, from the brain, goes down along the spinal cord in the sheath that covers the cord.

With the ebb and flow of this liquid, the movements of the bones of the skull are transmitted to the base of the spinal column, the sacrum. Sutherland named this phenomenon "primary respiratory movement," or "cranial-sacro respiration."

It is indeed at the levels of the skull and the sacrum (bottom part of the spinal column, fastening to the pelvis) that the osteopath best evaluates the harmony of this rhythmic movement.

The expression "primary respiratory movement" however is better fitting, since the starting point is the steady variation of volume within each of the billions of cells of a living body. Any cell lives by absorbing nurturing liquids, and expelling them back through its walls, with the residues due to its functioning. Concerning all the cells, this phenomenon amounts to a formidable stirring of the water held in the body—more than 80% of the total weight! That is why one can speak of ebb and flow.

All the cellular micro-pumps, whose effects add up, push rhythmically on the walls of the organism, and their action is more particularly felt in the places where hard walls are flush to the skin, which is the case for the skull and sacrum. At their level, the amplitude is still increased by the fact that they are linked to each other by a tube which is supple, but absolutely not elastic; this almost liquid tight tube is the "dura mater," which holds the cerebrospinal liquid. One may compare the movement of this liquid to a tide.

Considering only the starting points of the two osteopathic tendencies, one understands that the results are identical in both methods. A blocked vertebra entails the deformation of the meninges (dura mater) and hampers the circulation of the cerebrospinal liquid they hold. Structural osteopathy releases the vertebra and therefore liberates the circuit; fluidic osteopathy reinforces the current of the liquid and sweeps off the obstacle as it liberates the vertebra.

All the nuances exist between these two extreme tendencies of osteopathy. They, however, have the same purpose, and the same conception of the body's equilibrium.

I happen to use the techniques of cranial osteopathy in certain well-defined cases, particularly for some behavioral troubles and sometimes for ataxia (loss of balance) problems. Sacro-cranial manipulations are rather ticklish to implement with the animal for several reasons: the rhythm to evaluate is slower than with the human, but also it is physically impossible to palpate simultaneously the sacrum and the skull, unless two osteopaths work together (the comparison between the two extremities of the medullary canal is very useful for the diagnosis and treatment by this method).

Besides, an extensive training is necessary to learn how to palpate in each of these methods, and eventually one has to make a choice as to the basic technique.

There is an intermediary technique between the cranial approach and the structural approach: the fascial release method.

In anatomy, fascias are all the envelopes which delimit the diverse elements of a living body: it is about ligamentous "sheets" acting somewhat like sheaths. The best known are the muscular aponeuroses which one can see at a butcher's, as he is conditioning meat: they are those pearly envelopes which wrap up each muscle and must be removed before selling.

If two adjacent muscles can contract independently, it is because they both wear this perfectly slick "skin," furthermore lubricated by an intermediary liquid.

Upon a reflexive contracture of a muscular fascia, a partial adhesion of the aponeurosis happens, since the intermediary liquids were chased away by the compression resulting from the contracture. The fascial release technique amounts to separating manually the muscular masses in order to allow the return of the lubricating liquids.

This way of proceeding is akin to the massages of physiotherapy, but it insists more on the dissociation of the muscular masses than on their warming up.

Numerous "bone setters," sometime called "touchers," work in this way to release the muscular contractures of their clients. Their art lies all in the ability to detect instinctively the muscles to be separated from one another, yet without knowing anatomy.

To this, these same "touchers" often add an almost similar action, which has been called since "deep transverse massage," which consists of loosening up a contracted muscle through a strong massage of its extremity, where this muscle is fixed on the extending tendon. By making the tight muscle resound, a little as if it were a guitar string, one obtains its relaxation. A Canadian, Jack Meagher, inventoried all the points of the horse which are liable to be treated in this way and gets definite results in all the forms of contractures.

The technique of fascial release indeed figures among the set of osteopathic techniques since it liberates structural elements— i.e., the mucles—blocked against each other to allow the free circulation of the liquids.

All of these various techniques for treating a patient while abiding by the basic osteopathic concept set forth by Andrew Taylor Still are applicable to the horse and complement each other. While I do fascial release, deep transverse massage, and the cranial-sacro techniques when I deem them useful, I usually resort to the manual techniques, for which I have better feel for the majority of the cases I am presented with.

Furthermore, I believe that the brusque (I don't say brutal!) aspect of the manipulation induces a beneficial reflex arc which stimulates the nervous circuits affected by the lesion and sends the brain the clear message that the original spasm has yielded. Perhaps this is the reason why this method often brings definitive and at least more durable results.

Experience has shown me that, with the human as with the horse, the "fluidic" techniques, while beneficial, are perhaps too discreet to entail stable results alone. It is as if the induced reflex was too soft to erase in the brain the order of spasm installed since the appearance of the trouble.

Later on in this book I shall give a personal theory of the energetic action of osteopathy. This theory enables one to understand the basic structural manipulations. It in no way discards the fluidic techniques.

Bear in mind, that for equine and human osteopathy, the practitioner chooses the method which suits him/herself best to liberate all the blockings of the individual he/she must treat and therefore restores free circulation of fluids which, by flowing harmoniously, maintain the patient in good health.

Chapter 3

Structural manipulations

The technique I use with the horse refers to a reasoning pattern which is suited to the particular conformation and the temperament of this animal.

My way of explaining the osteopathic lesion, as well as the means to release it, is to be considered as a mental image of what happens, and not as a real fact, systematically present in every lesion.

I am going to use comparisons in an attempt to clarify, so this chapter should have as a title "Everything happens as if...."

The reasoning the theory entails easily shows the appropriate behavior in case of an unexpected locomotive problem. Therefore, this theory allows one to discover the ad hoc manipulation, and it also may be useful in the process of riding.

Health is a state of equilibrium, i.e., a state of constant oscillation between opposite tendencies which mutually balance each other. The functioning of a living organism is the result of antagonisms, from whichever angle one chooses to observe it:

• For western medicine, it is about the antagonism between the sympathetic and para-sympathetic nervous systems.

For Chinese medicine, it is the Yin-Yang equilibrium which can be found at every level.

As for osteopathy, it is about mechanical oscillation.

Indeed, when Andrew Taylor Still states that any structural element must be free, it means that this element should be able to oscillate unhampered around a medium position which is its normal anatomical position. Here again, one acknowledges the notion of oscillation I have mentioned and which defines life.

Imagine then a scale in a state of equilibrium; its beam oscillates constantly round the "zero point." Even if you do not really feel the movement of the beam, there nevertheless is one. A scale blocked on its equilibrium point would not allow one to weigh anything whatsoever, just as an organism blocked on its equilibrium point could not respond, nor adapt, to outside fluctuations. Such a situation bears a name: death.

The scale can also get immobilized in other positions, which we are going to examine. There are two possibilities for an obstacle opposing the freedom of the beam:

If the obstacle is situated *on the other side* of the beam with respect to the point of balance, this latter can oscillate, but only in a limited way. In the case of a living organism, it is about individuals who live well provided they lead a limited and tranquil life; some excesses are prohibited for them. Let's compare a joint to this balance: it allows only limited movements. There are therefore persons who, for years, have not been able to lift an arm higher than their shoulder. When it is about a blocking of the autonomic commands of one organ, we are dealing with so-called diseases of "insufficiency" (cardiac insufficiency, renal, hepatic, respiratory insufficiency, etc.). It is not about a real obstacle to the vital oscillations, but a limitation in their scope. This type of disease most often corresponds to the total or partial destruction of an organ, and one cannot do much more than try to avoid all excesses. One should have intervened before the destruction happened.

If the obstacle is placed *between* the beam and the point of balance, we are dealing with the most frequent case which will allow me to explain the osteopathic lesion: since the scale tends to return toward the point of balance, the beam pushes onto the obstacle and in doing so amplifies the blocking of the whole. It then becomes more difficult to remove the obstacle since the pressure of the beam sort of locks it.

The comparison with a scale is true for the whole organism, but likewise, this happens at the level of every organ and even every ligament, or bone, since Andrew Taylor Still discovered that they all should oscillate freely.

So when upon an excessive movement, an intervertebral joint (for instance) is at risk of trespassing the limits that it can afford, the nervous system reacts immediately through a spasm whose purpose is to avoid the worst. The vertebra then finds itself locked to its neighbor in its excessive position, but this position, however, still remains within permissible limits; the joint did not go so far as to get dislocated, thanks to the blocking.

If a vertebra can get blocked in this way, it is of course by means of the muscles which govern its joints. When a muscle or a ligament is overextended by a movement, its fellow antagonist tightens to a maximum, as if to withhold its congener for fear of it breaking. (To any muscle of the organism corresponds another muscle having the reverse action; we must have muscles to bend the arm, if others allow us to extend it. The antagonistic system is sometimes made of a ligament which acts as a passively repealing elastic.) This phenomenon hence does not apply only to vertebral joints, but also in any place where there are muscles, i.e., the whole organism.

Here I have to place a capital, although rather unexpected, notion:

The very painful spasm which accompanies the blockings is a phenomenon necessary to safeguard the integrity of the locomotive apparatus.

Without this safeguard, the individual wouldn't quit undergoing muscle and ligament disruptions. Said in a simple way, rejoice if your back hurts; this means that you were about to pull ligaments or muscles, and that your brain realized it in the nick of time. It ordered a spasm to counter the accident.

Why is this useful spasm so painful? Perhaps because if it were not, one would put up with it; but this situation better not last, lest it entail other troubles in other locations, as we will see later on.

Why, finally, doesn't the spasm yield on its own? Perhaps because the brain does not want to take the chance of lowering its "guard" in the event the excessive wrong position still exists. This happens, for instance, when the individual has one leg shorter than the other; one has to distinguish the "true" shorter leg, which is rare and due to a congenital malformation or the sequels of an ill-repaired fracture, from the "wrong" shorter leg which is very frequent and most often due to an easy to manipulate blocking of the pelvis.

Perhaps also because the local disorder of the relationship between the various structures mechanically prevents a return to normalcy. A ligament, for instance, may have interposed itself on the course which has to be liberated.

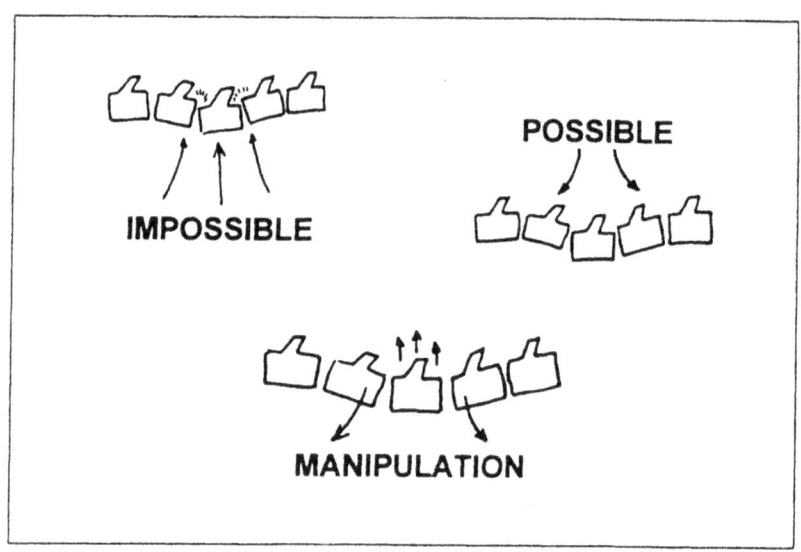

Finally, perhaps because the reflexes of safeguarding an organism are often disproportionate and excessive in order to meet the purpose more certainly. Daily life is filled with examples of exaggerated safeguarding reflexes: when one gets a finger burned, one withdraws violently one's arm, whereas most of the time, a half-inch withdrawal of the finger would have sufficed; allergic shocks are a good example of exaggerated reactions. Safeguard reactions seem to be excessive for fear of being insufficient.

Let's come back momentarily to our scale beam: on the occasion of an osteopathic lesion (blocking of a structural element), the ensemble tilted too much and the scale ended up blocked for safeguard purpose. One may then imagine that if the beam does not come back to its position of balance, it is because an obstacle has emerged which prevents its return. This obstacle is all the more firmly installed as the beam presses onto it in its attempt to come back toward normalcy.

Above, I alluded to a mental image one should bear in mind when one is confronted with an osteopathic lesion or a locomotive problem with the horse; this image, which gives the key for the release of a lesion, is very easy to grasp.

One just has to know how to release the hand brake of a car!

There is only one way to release a hand brake, and it takes almost no strength, even though the brake is tight enough to immobilize a vehicle from going downhill. If you press down onto the hand brake, it won't work; plus, you take the chance of breaking the mechanism if you are strong enough. If you merely try to press on the button on the tip of the brake handle, you are unlikely to succeed, and if so, it will be at the expense of the mechanism whose ratchet will wear out in time. To release the brake, everybody knows one has to move it in the only possible direction, which allows one, with a soft movement of the thumb, to unlock the ratchet and lower the handle.

I am not saying that any osteopathic lesion is mechanically withheld by a ratchet; this is merely a visual tool. Remember: "all works as if..." and thanks to this mental image, you will always figure out the appropriate mode of action.

Let us examine a typical example of an osteopathic lesion with a horse, and the ensuing manipulation according to this pattern:

When a blocking maintains a vertebral body in a **lowered position** with respect to its neighbors, the horse hollows his back and cannot lift his spinal column without increasing the pain.

The vertebrae on either side hold the affected vertebra in its wrong position and prevent its return to normalcy through a liberation of the spasm. The horse disengages its rear end, since it is the blocked vertebra which acts itself as a ratchet. Any attempt at lifting the back blocks the ratchet all the more.

The correct manipulation consists then of lowering briskly the affected segment of the spinal column. This movement, even if sometimes painful, opens the space between the two vertebrae squeezing the lesion; it releases the blocked vertebra (ratchet) which gets more than enough room to reintegrate to its normal position and retrieve its liberty of motion.

In the reverse case (vertebral body higher), the manipulation is as simple, but of course in the other direction.

For the blockings in a "latero-flexion" (vertebral body offset laterally), the pattern is still the same, but the manipulation is more difficult to achieve with the appropriate angle, since the "latero-flexions" (lateral bendings) are practically always compounded with a rotation of the vertebral body. It is then necessary to amplify the flexion by adding to it a movement of lifting, or lowering, of the back. The appropriate amplitude of the latero-flexions and of the flexions or extensions must be carefully calculated and realized.

As you see, the reasoning is easy as pie, and if one sticks to it while following the basic concept of Andrew Taylor Still, one can manipulate horses. The only, problem is to train oneself how to palpate in order to know what to manipulate, and in which direction.

I already stated that the horse won't tolerate our mistakes, but most of all we should bear in mind that one may trigger serious troubles if one forgets some lesions which were well compensated by the ensemble.

One risks revealing a serious lameness which the organism was obliterating through other lesions. Still more serious, as one attempts to solve in this way a locomotive trouble, one may trigger severe colic, an acute fit of emphysema, or any other accident which one won't be able to solve.

Practiced by persons without a solid formation in osteopathy, the structural manipulation is dangerous. It is the palpation, the "manual listening" which makes the difference. An American inquiry on the universal level did not reveal any major accident on humans manipulated by licensed osteopaths. It is a different case when the manipulators have not learnt how to palpate.

The picture gets more complex when one understands that a vertebra may seem to be in an abnormal position and still be free, whereas another may be in its normal place, but locked.

The osteopathic lesion is not measured with a ruler, or by reading an x-ray picture, it is felt with the hands, for its only definition is the loss of mobility.

I have in mind the case of a person affected with a total rigidity of the neck subsequent to a car accident. The x-ray picture showed a displacement of the fourth cervical vertebra; on the other hand, palpation revealed a blocking of the first three and the sixth cervical vertebrae.

The x-ray picture was certainly useful to eliminate any suspicion of fracture, but I leave it to your imagination to figure out what would have happened with a manipulation only based upon the radiological aspect of this blocked neck!

Chapter 4

Personal hypotheses on the mode of action

The individual confronted by the manipulations

For certain reasons, the horse is particularly suited for this alternative medicine known as osteopathy.

His autonomic nervous system is hypersensitive, and the variations of its balance are sudden and translate into spectacular reactions. Let it be remembered that the autonomic nervous system is made of all the nervous fibers which command the regulation of all the vital functions. Every organ receives nervous fibers of two types, the first ones accelerate its functioning, the others slow it down; the balance is the result of a constant oscillation from one effect to the other.

The importance of colic in the horse's pathology shows indeed the precariousness of this autonomic balance, and the uncommon amplitude of its variations.

With all mammals, the sympathetic fibers accelerate and strengthen the heart, but they slow the intestine and desiccate its content while increasing its role of re-absorption of the liquids it contains. The para-sympathetic fibers are responsible for the reverse phenomenon: they slow down the heart and lower the blood pressure, as they accelerate the intestine and the liquidity of its contents by an excess in the secretion of the glands in its wall. All animals are subjected to these variations, but only with the horse do they take on a variation in amplitude that is dangerous for the individual.

You should know that a horse can die out of pain when his digestive ligaments are sprained by a spasm of nervous origin. When a cow or a dog dies out of an intestinal occlusion, death occurs because the wall of the intestine is destroyed, whereas there are cases of horses dying without a lesion in the wall. The local stress of the nervous fibers may suffice to entail a deadly shock.

An animal whose autonomic nervous system is so sensitive in its reactions will respond even better to therapy which acts directly onto the commands of this system. It is therefore not surprising that osteopathy acts quickly and efficiently with the horse.

Another reason which predisposes a horse to being treated through osteopathy is the simplicity of his joints.

There is no other example with other mammals of such a simplification of the skeleton as with horses. Not only the joints of their members do not allow practically any rotation, but their spinal column is articulated in a simpler manner. Except at the level of the cervical vertebrae, the column of these animals authorizes only flexions (up-down, right-left) and does not allow torsions (the movement one does when one twists one's torso in order to look back.)

The limbs of the horse ending with one only "finger" which flexes only from front to rear also is an unique case of simplification.

These particularities create an animal, whose "chassis" is more stable and whose possible blockings are less complex. The articular manipulations of the horse with osteopathic lesions, are more rapidly efficient and stable than with any other species. I have often observed that one can obtain, in one session, healings which would require three or four with the human.

Finally, the equine offers a cutaneous hypersensitivity which allows one to make him easily "startle" by touching him at spots chosen in accordance with the movement one wants to foster. This latter peculiarity is very useful for the manipulation of animals endowed with such a large frame, the ratio of forces being to the disadvantage of the osteopath. One just has to place the horse in the position required by the manipulation, and then to trigger with one finger a reflex movement which releases the spasm responsible for the trouble. This technique is much less efficient with other, less reactive animals, like the bovine for instance.

All these positive elements have allowed me to progress rapidly in the elaboration of equine osteopathy, without pretending in any way that my approach is the only possible one. I am still far from having completely investigated the matter, but all the elements I have gathered to date open heretofore unsuspected horizons and sometimes cast a new light on the approach to the osteopathic concept.

More particularly, I'd like to propose two theories on the mode of action of the structural osteopathic treatment. The first theory deals with its repercussions at the level of the individual considered as a whole, and the second deals with what happens locally when we manipulate, and about the circuits which are put to work.

Above, I compared the osteopathic lesion to the handle of a tightened hand brake in order to explain the way to release it. Another way to say the same thing is to remark that the releasing consists of doing the same gesture as the gesture which created the blocking. The former is softer than the latter and goes hardly farther. Now consider carefully this pattern, and you will find out that it is pretty much reminiscent of the homeopathic approach.

With homeopathy, the individual is administered the very product which will bring about the same symptoms. It is kind of pushed a little farther into its trouble to get out of this trouble. This is done in a controlled, non-noxious manner, and all the genius of Dr. Samuel Christian Frederic Hahnemann M.D. (1755-1843), the founder of homeopathy, lies in the discovery of this therapeutic means.

But the horses I have treated have led me to push this reasoning further. When a horse presents osteopathic lesions subsequent to a fall, and if these lesions turn him practically into an invalid (slanted neck, stiff back, lameness, etc.), there is a way to release all the lesions in one stroke. It consists of setting the spinal column of the horse in the position it was in during the fall!

This is conceivable theoretically but seems hardly feasible practically, though it is sometimes possible since the animal lends itself rather freely to it. The horse accompanies the positioning gestures and even directs them, since other gestures have become mechanically impossible for him.

This finding is in evidence with cervical accidents entailing "stiff neck" like troubles. For instance, if the horse has fallen with his head under his shoulder, the manipulation which will heal him is done by flexing his neck in this very position, and then in reinforcing slightly this malposition.

This technique is valid even if the cervical segment offers several different blockings.

I just compared osteopathy to homeopathy; one might as well compare it to another therapy of the stresses undergone by an individual: psychoanalysis.

One may disagree with some psychologists, but it is undeniable that psychoanalysis has helped numerous persons in overcoming events of their lives they could not assume. The psychoanalytic "manipulation" is more difficult to implement, because it is not mechanical and therefore not amenable to measurements or at lease is difficult to control in its amplitude.

The fact remains that in psychoanalysis, one speaks of "unblocking," "unclenching," "freeing" an individual.

A structural osteopathic manipulation consists of helping the patient to confront the stress which could not be assumed and which provoked the blocking, but this in a controlled environment, devoid of danger, pushing even a little further, to help the patient *assess* the problem, be reassured, and quit being blocked.

Sometimes it may be useful to have beforehand a fairly precise description of the accident which created the trouble, in order to manipulate an individual efficiently. But more often, it goes the other way around. When the osteopath is experienced and knows how to palpate all the lesions with finesse, it is he/she who happens to describe the accident nobody ever witnessed (wherever it took place, in the stall or in a field).

With this respect, the manipulation follows somewhat the pattern of psychoanalysis, irrespective of any question of duration. The patient experienced a stress which he/she only knows about (even if it has been forgotten), and the therapist, simply by listening, guides him/her toward the conditions which will help him/her to confront this stress. In the lines here above, I mentioned the expression "manual listening." This comparison with psychoanalysis shows that it fits quite well.

It is indeed the very same image which comes back in several domains relating to the health and balance of an individual. The imbalance is due to too strong an aggression which paralyzed some functions with the victim, a victim who can get out of it only by "reliving" the same event in a calming environment, ruling out any reaction of panic.

The circuits of action of the manipulations

Structural osteopathy is indicated for dysfunctions of the locomotive apparatus, but also in numerous organic or functional internal troubles. This statement displeases vertebro-therapeutist physicians who manipulate the spinal column in order to treat backaches originating in the vertebrae, but don't acknowledge any extended pathological action.

When one of their patients tells them that a manipulation suppressed his/her digestive troubles, they attribute it to the placebo effect, or to the lessening of the anxiety resulting from the pain.

Everybody acknowledges now that a vertebral blocking may act at a distance and bring about a phenomenon of pain on the course of the nerve affected by the lesion. This is the case especially with the sciatic neuralgia, which may sometimes manifest itself through an ache in the foot only. In this case, the dysfunction of a sensory and motor nerve is due to a vertebral lesion, and is perceived only far from this lesion. Even if a local anesthesia confirms that indeed the foot is the location of the pain, it is only by treating the vertebral lesion that one will take care of the problem.

Why should the peripheral dysfunction of a nerve injured at the vertebral level apply only to sensory or motor nerves and not to nerves of the autonomic system?

The autonomic nervous fibers are also affected by vertebral blocking. They even are affected in the first place since every sensory or motor nerve is wrapped in a sheath made of autonomic fibers! Speaking of a sciatic nerve blocked by a vertebral lesion does not mean that this nerve presses against the bone, for that would definitely destroy it. As a matter of fact, it is compressed by the edema of its sheath, and this edema is due to the irritation of the autonomic fibers which surround it.

It has been discovered recently that the intervertebral disc itself is innervated with autonomic fibers; now this disc is the first to be affected by a malposition of a blocked vertebra.

One may picture the fibers of the autonomic nervous system like an entanglement of a multitude of spider webs wrapping all the parts of the organism; and this network stems from the spinal cord and therefore from the vertebral joints. Any abnormality in the relationship between two elements of the organism affects first and foremost the autonomic nervous fibers, these latter perturbing in turn the blood circulation they regulate the flow of.

When the functioning of an autonomic nerve is perturbed, the organ this nerve assures the regulation of by maintaining the balance between the two phases "sympathetic" and "para-sympathetic" cannot fulfill its function.

This obvious reasoning is verified every day in osteopathy. There are numerous problems, whether digestive, cardiac, respiratory, renal, and even hormonal, which are only due to an osteopathic vertebral lesion and which can easily be treated and healed osteopathically.

Furthermore, the joints are so much simpler with the horse that the connection between an intervertebral joint and an organ is precise; I have been able to establish a chart of the troubles linked to each vertebra. For instance, I can affirm that ovary troubles are linked to the lesions of the first lumbar vertebra, and this is confirmed by the results of osteopathic manipulations.

The whole concept becomes more complex when the osteopaths, having succeeded in convincing some non-believers that a blocked vertebra can perturb an organ, also affirm that this process works both ways, and that the dysfunction of an organ entails rapidly a corresponding vertebral locking!

This reversed connection is as frequently observed, but is much more reluctantly accepted by western, Cartesian minds. Here again, I affirm, however, that a trouble which starts at the ovary of a mare induces almost certainly a blocking of the first lumbar.

The healing of the ovary through a classic allopathic treatment will liberate the vertebral spasm without one having to worry about it, but I have also proved that the reciprocal held true.

Some osteopaths explain the action of an organic trouble on some level of the spinal column by saying that the disease perturbs all of the autonomic course between the organ and the related intervertebral spasm and creates a weak point on this latter. Then, by the slightest wrong movement, the vertebra will block itself. Nobody has ever found a way to break another link than the weak one while pulling on a chain, so the same pattern would hold true for the spinal column.

A reasoning based on the tenets of traditional Chinese acupuncture allows an explanation of this phenomenon but could hardly convince western minds who discard this mode of thinking.

The meridians of acupuncture have been set in evidence thanks to radioactive markers, and one has had the confirmation that they do not follow any known anatomic tissue. Their courses, therefore, have no material support and yet are real in their existence and their topography. Research has discovered that these meridians were following the lines of magnetic fields. The flowing energy of the Chinese would be made of electromagnetic waves guided by those fields.

In structural osteopathy, the manipulations which best re-equilibrate the internal state of an individual, address the joints situated on the so called "energy command points" of the various meridians of acupuncture. The intervertebral joints are right beneath the SHU[4] points of the meridians, whereas the joints of the limbs house the "antique" points. These special "antique" points increase, lessen, or change the course of the energy in each meridian.

The osteopathic manipulation performed in one of those areas works on the quantity and quality of energy in the related meridian; this may be verified by checking the pulses or with the help of electric testers.

What then are those joints which, situated on the course of the Energy (electromagnetic wave), are able to influence it by deterioration or a stabilization?

The state of the art technique in electronics includes and has used for some years a very reliable system of oscillating circuits which presents the advantage of not spending additional energy (in the Western sense); it is about the regulation by quartz, based on the so-called piezo-electric effect.

Here is the dictionary's definition:

"Piezo-electricity: appearance of electric charges on the surface of some materials when they are submitted to a constraint (direct effect), or conversely, variation of the dimensions of these materials upon application of an electrical tension (reverse effect)."

---

4   Chinese name for these points

The piezo-electrical effect is routinely used for the regulation of "electronic" wrist watches: an electronic circuit creates the most stable oscillations possible for the functioning of the watch, but these oscillations would vary anyway due to variations of temperature; they have to be regulated by quartz. So one sets on the course of the oscillating circuit a crystal of quartz whose thickness is determined by its own length of wave which has to match this to the oscillations one wants to stabilize. The oscillations resulting from this combination are invariable thanks to the piezo-electric effect.

The crystal of quartz can also transform mechanical energy into electrical oscillating energy, as is the case with flintless lighters. Striking a crystal of quartz creates an electrical tension between its two faces and produces a spark. The electric current so induced is an alternating current, the polarity shifting at the rhythm of the vibrations of the crystal.

A last detail one has to know about the "piezo-electric" effect is that if one sends toward a crystal of quartz an oscillating circuit whose frequency differs too much from this corresponding to its thickness, the crystal will be deformed and may even deteriorate.

Do you see what I am pointing at?

The living organism is permeated by an energy conveyed by oscillating circuits along magnetic fields. In addition, these circuits are constantly regulated, tuned up, and reinforced by "quartzes:" the joints.

When one of these articular "quartzes" is deformed out of a compression due to a spasm, the corresponding meridian is out of tune, the trains of waves reaching the concerned organ cannot assure its normal activity anymore.

The manipulation of this articular quartz has a double effect: its liberates the quartz, thus giving it the possibility to vibrate anew at the proper frequency; plus, the shock so in flicted upon it sends into the circuit a beneficial train of waves, because it is perfectly tuned to the proper frequency.

Finally and especially, one understands then how an ailing organ itself emitting out of tune frequencies in the meridian may deform the quartz and block it.

This theory offers the advantage of corresponding to what can be observed on a practical plane, but like all theories, it works only as long as one has not found a better one. Scientific progress is made only by climbing a ladder whose steps are the successive theories answering a common question, in the light of new details.

This approach to the self-regulation of living organisms sets an important notion in evidence: One certainly moves because one is alive, but first and foremost one is alive because one moves!

All the movements we make, if only breathing, solicit joints which, besides the mobility they allow, constantly recharge our circuits. Movement transforms mechanical energy into vital energy in order to compensate for the inevitable losses.

Old age brings about diverse arthritis[5] and conversely arthritis begets aging by suppressing the efficacy of a great number of "articular quartzes."

Arthritis is only a degeneration, a clogging up of the piezo-electric systems the organism is equipped with. It is the articular blocking, which holds up the blood circulation and therefore induces arthritis; when one sets an obstacle in a river, alluvial deposits come up. Arthritis is the alluvial deposit resulting from the stagnation of energy.

Therefore, instead of saying: "It's normal you can't move, you have arthritis," I'd rather tell you: "It's normal you have arthritis, since your joints do not move!"

The manipulation of arthritic joints is delicate, and must be executed with competence, but its repetition lessens the arthritis, as has been often noticed. The restoration of the blood and energy circulation it brings about drains the lesions by carrying the alluvial deposits away.

---

5   Arthritis: joint deterioration caused by trophic degeneration.

Chapter 5

Life

The horses treated through osteopathy have given me a plausible answer to a problem which concerns all humans since their arrival on Earth; they gave me a way to understand the process of aging.

It is obviously about only one of the aspects of the aging process which every living creature undergoes, but it allows one to understand why today's medicine still can't help much about it; and to better explain my point of view, I shall tell you here the story of a horse. It is not about an isolated case. I have often dealt with such pathological patterns, but I simply chose one to support my thesis.

But let us first come up with a few remarks on the actual possible options of medicine with respect to the aging process, by quoting a great American osteopath, Professor Irvin M. Korr: "Allopathic Medicine knows how to add years to the life, but not how to add life to the years."

Korr is dealing here with chronic diseases which are the true cause of aging.

Statistics may be misleading. Medicine prides itself, and rightfully so, on having increased the life expectancy of the diseased through the progress it has made in the recent decades, but this statistical improvement is due to the solutions it has brought about in a truly other domain than aging.

In fact, more people than before are likely to grow older only because fewer children are dying at an early age from acute diseases. Medicine certainly has increased the number of adults with respect to the number of births.

Korr lets us notice that, whereas the percentage of individuals over 60 has doubled in forty years of progress, the life expectancy of the 60 year old man, by contrast, is the same as the life expectancy of a 60 year old man in the year 1900!

Quoting Korr again: "...the overcoming of major infectious diseases has confronted mankind with problems at least as serious for which no solution has yet been found." Medicine adds years to life, because its only resource with chronic diseases is to chemically or surgically suppress the affected organs, and above all to teach the diseased to live differently, to slow his/her activities. It is at the cost of a more and more restricted and assisted life that the "patient" lasts longer. Before today's medicine, people would die when they could no longer be active by themselves. It is certainly a process, which is statistically compounded by the fact that there are more adults, but this conceals the real problem: modern medicine has not healed the chronic diseases which create aging!

Furthermore, physicians do not know how to prevent them. The only prevention is to fend off their initial causes through a better hygiene of life before they come about; but as soon as a lesion comes up, its evolution is inescapable.

People object that death is inevitable. But anyone would also agree that it would be preferable to die as old but also as alive as possible.

I think that, actually, treating chronic disease as we do amounts to bringing cookies to the prisoner while leaving him in the hands of his torturers. Indeed, with chronic diseases, you will find out that the organ which cries is rarely the culprit; it is instead, a victim, and the culprit is always unassuming when there is a victim and a culprit. Medicine deals only with the victim, and even ends up killing it surgically by removing it.

I am not criticizing surgery and I admire its achievements, I simply feel sorry that there is no other recourse.

So, here is now the story of this horse, which says much in a very simple way. It is about a sport horse whose owners were very fond of him. Upon stepping on an outcropping stump in a forest lane, he sprained his rear right ankle.

It was a very big sprain that the veterinarian diagnosed, and the horse could not even lean on his right hind leg for five days. The appropriate local treatment allowed him to stand again on it, and it took a month to dissipate the reaction of the tissues and bring this ankle back to its usual look. However, in spite of this therapeutic success, the horse remained slightly lame and no treatment could overcome this sequel.

The veterinarian in charge observed abnormal connections between the bones of the pelvis and had the horse sent to me with a little note summing up the story and the treatment which had been administered.

After having verified myself that the ankle was presenting a quite normal aspect, and did not react in pain to the usual tests, I confirmed the lesion of the pelvis, a sacro-iliac subluxation.

I concluded, as the treating veterinarian had, that this was the consequence of the sprain, a secondary lesion which then had to be dealt with, which I did through the appropriate manipulation.

Five days later, the owner made another appointment and brought me back his horse, a very lame horse whose sprain had, however, been healed four months earlier!

The cause for the lameness was obvious, it was indeed an apparently recent ankle sprain, and yet the horse had only been walked in hand!

The original sprain had therefore not been healed, in spite of the appearances, and the manipulation of the pelvis had removed the compensating lesion. This compensation had been effectual clinically (restored support and only slight trace of lameness) as well as cosmetically (suppression of the inflammation and return to a normal shape).

The subsequent treatment of the sprain succeeded thoroughly, since the equilibrium of the skeleton had been restored.

The art, for a good osteopath, lies in feeling such a lesion as this ankle in spite of its normal appearance and treating it as well as the pelvic compensatory problem.

This pattern is also known with humans. Particularly, little does one imagine the long term consequences of a sprained ankle, and it is not rare that individuals complain about cervical pains or even recurring migraines without establishing a connection with the ankle sprained a few years earlier. I am not saying that all migraines are due to this, but some are. Those will quit at an osteopath's who, having understood that one treats the whole individual and not a symptom, discovered the hidden lesions of the sprain and healed them.

If one manipulates only the cervical vertebrae, the result will be very momentary; if indeed one treats the whole column and especially the pelvis, without checking the ankles, the symptoms of the sprain will reappear in time, in spite of the months or years past since its healing.

This explains also why there are persons who twist constantly the same foot for all their life after an initial sprain.

This pathological pattern, often established and subsequently verified by the success of a skillful osteopathic treatment, leads me to propose a hypothesis on one of the modes of aging.

The newborn is, theoretically, deprived from any chronic lesion, a state which may last quite some time.

Someday, accidentally or subsequent to an acute disease, an important lesion appears in his organism, a lesion whose gravity is such that it is unbearable and incompatible with a normal life. This lesion translates, according to the osteopaths, into a structural osteopathic lesion and affects the tension of ligaments and some joint, in the broad sense of this term. The organism would be in much danger if it had to wait until this local problem is healed in order to resume the main activities which allow life to go on. It therefore chooses another solution, much more efficient in the short term.

The initial lesion is rarely completely healed; its noxious effects disappear because the organism breaks down the problem into so many other bearable lesions, compatible with the vital functions, and whose sum equals the initial stress.

The other lesions so installed will originate in turn as many little local circulatory troubles with apparently minute but chronic consequences. Especially, they induce the settling in of the unobtrusive phenomena of arthritis.

In addition, and above all, these small lesions will subsequently be so many weak points predisposing to another serious accident. This new stress will be absorbed in the same way by the organism which wants to live at all cost, and this will spawn still other minute lesions, weakening the whole.

Old age will then sneak in with its host of chronic diseases, arthritis, and induced organic deficiencies, since "structure rules function."

Death will come the day when the organism has exhausted all its possibilities of compensation.

The process may be very fast, if every lesion is compensated by four or five which someday become severe enough to be compensated each by as many others. The pace of aging differs from one individual to another.

All considered, nature is fairly well-organized as it certainly is a good solution to annul a big and unbearable accident and replace it with numerous small ones. But the account is strictly held, and try as we may to prevent it, saturation happens in the end.

Unlike allopathic medicine, osteopathy knows how to slow the saturation process and prolong life.

For this purpose, osteopathic medicine has to be the most preventive possible; it must intervene with each accident, whether mechanical or infectious. (This, of course, does not exclude resorting to allopathy in order to kill the germ which takes advantage of the situation; one should not discard that which has proven effective.)

If the osteopath cannot suppress the compensations of a lesion he can't cure, these lesions will return.

If, as is possible for many accidents of daily life, the osteopath suppresses the compensations as well as the lesion which induced them, the countdown to death will be slowed. Above all death will be faced in better health, even though this statement may seem paradoxical. Nobody dreams of spending fifteen years in a nursing home in assisted care.

Still, an individual who spent several years of his life with unbearable migraines before getting rid of them by an osteopath will have spent more of his supply of life than the one whose sprain and associated compensations were treated as soon as the accident occurred.

This, the chiropractors don't know, as I have established several times. They know very well how to manipulate, but they take care only of the sore locus, as they have not learned how to examine the whole organism or to palpate it, to listen to it as osteopaths do. They do not know that, as I wrote in the lines above, the organ which cries is a victim, not the culprit. Or if they know it, they don't take it into consideration in their practice. The osteopaths know it, and the time is overdue to rally all those skills and approaches together.

And since I think that it is difficult to be simultaneously at the top of all the allopathic and osteopathic therapies, all these people have to set to working together rather than criticizing each other.

I am already sure that it will be done faster in equine than in human medicine.

Since the horse helped me in understanding much on osteopathy, its mode of action and its therapeutic possibilities, it is only fair that he benefit from it.

The following chapters deal with what this kind of medicine brings to the treatment of the pathophysiology of the horse and his performance.

Part Two: The Horse Seen From An Osteopathic Point Of View

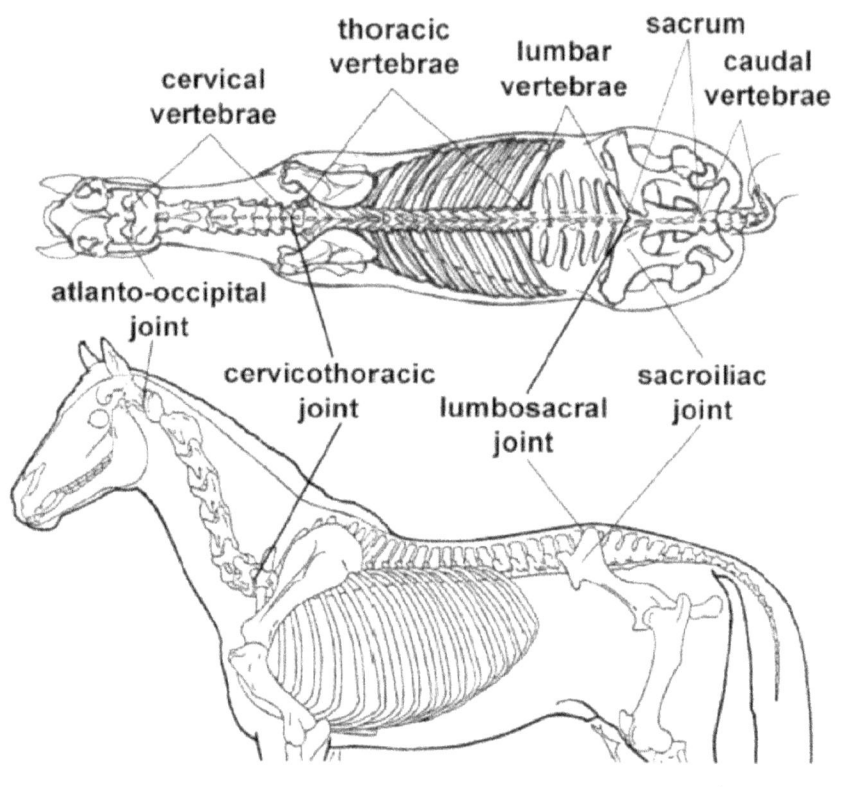

[The chart above is included for reference and convenience and is new to the 2014 edition. *Editor's note.*]

Chapter 6

The vertebra-organ link

This chapter concerns even those who don't intend to become equine osteopaths. It allows diagnosing a fair number of medical problems through a mere exam of the vertebral column.

Osteopathy is not the only therapeutic road; besides, it does not allow one to treat everything, though it can be the choice method in many cases. Undoubtedly, it brings very efficient help in diagnosing varrious afflictions.

The link between an injured vertebra and the trouble of the corresponding organ is more binding with horses than with men. I adopt the term "link" since, as I explained, one cannot know beforehand which problem came first.

By examining the back of an animal, the osteopath can give very precise indications about the whole health and behavior of the patient.

Not only can he describe the attitude of the horse while working or in his stall, but he also discovers rapidly sometimes unsuspected troubles the horse is suffering from.

The following list is not exhaustive. It is always growing. But here I describe what I have been abel to verify often enough to allow me to speak with certainty.

One can't help being surprised for the first time as one sees a person running a hand over the back of a horse s/he doesn't know, saying without bending over: 'Your horse has a retracted testicle whose cord is sore!" Yet there is no mystery involved, since a blocking of the first lumbar vertebra almost infallibly accompanies this problem.

Before starting the list, a little detail has to be pointed out: one may find vertebral lesions which are not accompanied with the symptom one expects. This can happen when the vertebral lesion is mechanically very well-compensated by another. It is precisely in such a case that if one manipulates only the compensation, one creates problems which may possibly be serious. For this reason, let's repeat: it is dangerous to manipulate a horse without having the right palpation training, which can only be acquired slowly.

Chapter 7

The sacrum

The sacrum is the base part of the spinal column, built of several vertebrae welded together, and articulating with the pelvic bones. In this chapter, I am going to explain the anatomy. But don't worry, it's going to be simple.

Although the spinal cord ends at the level of the second lumbar vertebra, the nerves stemming from it go further down through the vertebral canal and exit the sacrum through symmetrical holes. These holes in a bone have a fixed diameter and hence cannot "pinch" a nerve.

On the other hand, blocking one of the sacro-iliac joints (which link the sacrum to the pelvis) deforms the ligaments of the pelvis and strains the local muscles, between which the nerves are running. This brings up perturbations in the functioning of the sciatic, crural, and "pudic" nerves (from the Latin *pudere*, to be ashamed) nerves. The pudic nerves relate to the genitalia and were so named in the Middle Ages by the monks who redacted the books of anatomy, since only they knew how to write!

Irritations of these sacral nerves disrupt the equilibrium of the whole spinal column since it is through the sacrum that the propulsion of the hind legs is transmitted to the rest of the chassis.

Sacral irritations and imbalances cause locomotive problems which are not necessarily painful, but whose cause is mechanical. These lesions often cause the croup to be tipped to one side.

The horse is reluctant to bend to the side of the lower haunch, since he then would have to rotate his pelvis in the other direction. Such a horse fusses about letting the farrier hold the leg on the higher side because this tends to increase the already existing deviation of his pelvis (blocked at the sacrum).

In addition to this mechanical problem, the strain on the sacro-iliac ligaments causes a sciatic neuralgia on the side of the higher haunch. This confirms what anybody can observe, that a horse turns less freely toward the side opposed to the limb affected with a sciatic pain.

An important peculiarity of this kind of sciatica is that such a horse often gets a capped hock on the affected leg (that of the higher haunch). In this case the pain in the sciatic nerve does not depend on the movements of the spinal column unlike the lumbar originated sciaticas. Therefore the pain is as important (if not stronger) at a rest as in motion. The contraction of the muscles of the buttock in a standing position compresses the nerve, and the horse kicks in his stall to get rid of the pain. This type of sciatica, which hurts more when sitting in an armchair than while walking, is known by humans as well.

Many other symptoms are caused by sacral asymmetries.

One observes cases of pneumo-vagina (partial paralysis and distension of the walls of the vagina which draws in air as the horse is working); partial paralyses of the rectum which remains full of fecal droppings, these latter being expelled only by the thrust of defecation later. I have been able to solve two cases of paralysis of the penis.

But this does not mean that every paralysis proceeds from a blocking of the sacrum. The same is true for all the symptoms described in this chapter.

The blocking of the sacrum is almost always associated with a faulty carriage of the tail, but the reverse is not always true. Osteopathic lesions of the sacrum have a traumatic origin; they may be very old and date back from the time the colt was romping in the fields with his peers.

By pulling up on his halter, a horse combines two important causes of blocking of the sacrum: the fall onto his croup, and the traction on the poll by the halter, transmitted to the sacrum by the "dura-mater," the envelope of the spinal cord, which is not elastic and is not fixed to the vertebrae, but only to the skull and the sacrum.

The most frequent cause of lesions is the fact that we leave the horse in his stall twenty three hours out of twenty four. For lack of room, the horse cannot roll over on the ground without getting cast against a wall. His efforts to get back onto his feet are made at the expense of his spinal column, which is little designed for twisting.

A horse you find cast in his stall doesn't have any lesions yet, or very few, but the horse who succeeded in standing back up from a very bad position is rarely intact in this respect. Therefore it may happen that your horse comes out of his stall with a bending problem he didn't have the day before.

One unexpected cause of blocking of the sacrum (or "sacro-iliac subluxation") is the rushing through the stall door, when a horse violently bumps his hip against the door post. This may unsettle the pelvis with respect to the sacrum and trigger a rebellious sciatica.

Chapter 8

The lumbar vertebrae

There are six lumbar vertebrae with most horses. The interesting exceptions are the Barb, who have only five, as well as donkeys, mules, and sometimes Arabians. All the motor nerves stemming from the lumbar vertebral spaces provide branches to the sciatic nerve, so their lesions are always accompanied with a more or less important sciatic component.

When a lumbar vertebra is blocked, the horse goes crooked in his gaits.

Besides the cervical vertebrae, those are the only vertebrae which tolerate some twisting around the axis of the column. This allows a horse to swing his hind legs sideways while clearing a jump. This rotation of the lumbar vertebrae is, as well, the only means allowing the lateral work in dressage. The horse, indeed, has an additional ligament in the hip joint which prevents him from moving a hind leg off to the side; he, therefore, can do it only by tipping off his pelvis through a rotation of the lumbar vertebrae around their longitudinal axis. It is finally this very possibility of twisting which limits damages when a horse gets cast against the walls of his stall.

Thus, Barb horses are more fragile in the stall. Their shorter lumbar segment gives them more power to carry weight, but on the other hand, this diminishes their twisting capabilities. Therefore, these horses are more prone to blocking their last thoracic vertebra whose range of motion is limited by its being hooked onto the rib cage. Like the mule or the donkey, these are horses more resilient at work, but who should not be cramped into small boxes.

The sixth lumbar vertebra is linked to troubles of the bladder, which spasms when this vertebra is blocked, so the horse can't urinate well and never empties his bladder completely. He suffers from retention and accumulates poisonous toxins. This sometimes results in stocked up hind legs.

Mares may combine the lesions of the bladder to an inflammation of the neck of the womb, with spasm and varied infections. I have seen cases of mares offering discharges rebellious to all treatments immediately healed upon manipulation of the last lumbar. Even when the discharges have a bacterial origin, an antibiotic is inefficient as long as the vertebral lesion remains. Manipulation, by contrast, restores the local circulation to a sufficient extent for the organism to get rid of the bacteria by itself. This occurs on other vertebral levels of the organism. I therefore won't repeat it; I bid the non-believers to verify this for themselves.

Blocking of the sixth lumbar is generally manifested by a pelvic torsion leading to sciatica. A horse affected with such a lesion tends to "cross canter."

The lesion may also occur via an extension, meaning that the vertebra is pushed down with respect to the others. This is a very frequent case with the steeplechaser who sometimes lands on all fours after jumping like a deer, hence forcing this vertebra downward. Such a horse remains stretched out and refuses to engage his rear end.

For the fourth and fifth lumbar vertebra, I haven't yet discovered any particular pattern of pathology. From an osteopathic point of view, it is certainly one of those two which is missing in the Barb. They may very well get blocked and are then linked to a sciatic or crural neuralgia with a local "lumbago" type pain.

The third lumbar, besides locomotion problems, is associated to intestinal perturbations such as diarrhea. Even if one has the proof that the diarrhea started from a totally different cause, if the trouble persists in spite of allopathic treatments, it is very likely that the vertebra responded with a lesion which, although itself a consequence, was enough to maintain the symptom.

I think that this action is due foremost to an imbalance of the autonomic fibers regulating the glandular secretions in the intestine. Indeed, even if there is no diarrhea, the feces are foul-smelling and an input of digestive ferments in the feed makes up momentarily for the problem. The modification of the intestinal secretions certainly destroys the intestinal flora.

I do not count any longer the cases of chronic diarrhea healed by the mere manipulation of this vertebra, one of the latest to date being that of a horse brought to me by a fellow veterinarian. The horse had been afflicted with this trouble for six years, and the veterinarian, although at first skeptical like everybody, called me over the phone one month later to tell me that the feces had come back to normalcy the day after the manipulation!

Another aspect of the blocking of L3 is its connection with ligament problems in the patella. It is amazing to notice that in homeopathy, "Gelsemium" which treats some diarrheas is also indicated for numerous patellar problems.

The second lumbar is associated with the kidneys. If the lesion has been present for some time, one may assume that the horse carries an abnormal degree of urea. It is very often accompanied with a blocking of L6, which links together renal and bladder pathologies.

The second lumbar is the vertebra responsible for most cases of lumbar myositis of the galloper. Great stars of the race track have given me another, mechanical explanation which can be easily verified. With the standard quality Thoroughbred, the engagement of the hind legs under the body during the final sprinting stretch is such that the flexion of the lumbar vertebrae overwhelms their range of motion. When the hind legs are in their foremost position, the extreme curvature of the back is at the level of the second lumbar, and a blocking may occur at this place. At first, it is a lesion by simple flexion, and everything comes back to normalcy after a few days of muscular contraction if the horse at rest. If he is galloped again during this period for his training, the lesion will compound itself with a rotation, and is subsequently very little likely to heal on its own. It will be said later on that the horse has not recuperated well from his race or his work, and one has to wait until he gets rid of this lesion or compensates it, which will usually impair his performance.

The first horse to have "explained" this trouble to me was so exceptional that he required a manipulation of L2 every other, or every three canters. The year before he was exposed to this type of therapy, he had performed very well but had not been raced often due to frequent myositis.

If you come across a young horse who blocks his L2 in flexion upon being galloped, keep tabs on him!

The first lumbar vertebra is very important to the horse's reproductive function. It concerns the testicles in the male and the ovaries in the mare. These glands, moreover, have the same autonomic innervation since they were not differentiated at the start of embryomic development.

LI is linked to ovarian dysfunctions in the mare and is found to be in a state of imbalance when there are ovarian insufficiencies (undeveloped ovaries, lack of hormonal secretions), as well as in cases of ovary hyperfunctioning (inflammations, cysts, nymphomania). Manipulating has a good effect on these diverse troubles, but the vertebral blocking will reappear if one ovary is definitively damaged. Such is the case with fibrocystic ovaries which should have been dealt with much earlier.

I believe that many cystic ovaries have become so because of a previous fibrocystic blocking of the first lumbar, whether of traumatic origin or due to a reflex subsequent to an ovarian inflammatory process. In the male, I have not been in a position to study any possible link with hormonal function since I didn't treat breeding stallions. I would not be surprised if there were a link between LI and libido or fertility, but this remains to be verified.

The association between this lesion and testicular torsions or testicle cord retraction problems is very apparent. Chronic torsions of a testicle happen with young horses. Their manual release is greatly facilitated if one first manipulates the first lumbar; then recurrence becomes rarer.

I have seen cases of four year old horses where "ill descended" testicles would complete their migration within two weeks after a manipulation. Moreover, this is well-documented in children.

I will finally note that geldings which are bothered by a castration scar react to this problem through a blocking of the first lumbar. In these cases, the surgical adhesions must be removed. These troubles cease upon release of the vertebral blocking and its possible compensations.

Chapter 9

The thoracic vertebrae

A horse has eighteen thoracic vertebrae. Each of them is articulated with a pair of ribs.

The eighteenth thoracic is associated with troubles of the large intestine and particularly with stasis colic (constipation). Horses who show this colic repeatedly should be examined carefully at T18. If T18 is indeed in a state of lesion, manipulating takes care of this type of chronic trouble once and for all.

The symptoms one observes are related to a stimulation of the orthosympathetic system. Its nervous fibers are in charge of slowing the intestinal transit and increasing the absorption of the water and liquid nutrients remaining in the colon subsequently to the digestion of the food. When these nervous fibers are irritated by the blocking of the last thoracic, their action is strengthened, resulting in a stagnation in the intestine of a more and more desiccated matter. This stasis colic corresponds to constipation with the human.

From a locomotive point of view, this blocking is typical of horses who roll in their stalls. The twisting of the lumbar vertebrae resulting from this gesture cannot be transmitted to the thoracic vertebrae, which display a limited range of rotation due to their connection to the ribs. It is unfortunate for those horses that the very vertebra related to the stasis colic happens to be the most vulnerable when a horse rolls, and this may explain why some heretofore perfectly sound horses may all of a sudden become prone to repeated colic after a first fit which made them roll much. Serious colic may bring about spinal lesions which correlate to the digestive tube or its appendages, and the reoccurrence is then facilitated. While these noxious lesions indeed exist, I think that there are first and foremost thoracic sequels due to the wrong movements of the horse struggling in his stall, as proven by the results of the manipulation.

I am not aware of association of T17 and T16 with definite particular pathology. Some cases, however, have led me to think that T17 might be related to the adrenal glands. These glands are in charge of secreting diverse hormones, including cortisol (secreted by the body itself). The adrenals are involved with the distribution of the body liquids and are sometimes associated with edema problems.

The blocking of these vertebrae results in difficulties in lateral bending as well as in a quasi-impossibility to maintain the horse on a straight line, since he has to be more or less "crooked" in order to move forward. This fact is most disturbing with the Standardbred whose symmetry in the gaits must be as perfect as possible in order to avoid "clipping."

The fifteenth thoracic vertebra, besides offering the same locomotive symptom as the two previous ones, is typical of horses whose autonomic system is off balance by an excess of "para-sympathetic" tone. These animals sweat abnormally and may offer a second fit of sweat in their stall, although they were dry when they walked into it. They are emotional and are prone to stasis colic as well as brutal and brief diarrheas. Unlike the sympathetic, these para-sympathetic fibers activate the excretory systems and accelerate the movements of the intestine.

The fourteenth thoracic is very rarely blocked; it is rather the setting of a very localized muscular contracture. This contracture in T14 is the rule in case of hepatic troubles. The affection of the liver may be due to a lot of different causes (intoxication, worms, viral attack), but the resulting muscular tension is the same.

The stomach and its troubles are revealed by T13, T12, and sometimes T11. It may range from frequent yawning to wind sucking (cribbing), to perturbations of taste and appetite. Contrarily to what one may think initially, an insatiable horse may be so because of stomach pain. He understands that a full stomach hurts less than an empty one.

In case of obvious gastric troubles, one should always think of possible parasitism and seek information about the date of the last worming and brand name of the wormer.

T10 to T3 make up the area of the withers and may be connected to some pulmonary and cardiac troubles, but their impact is for the most part essentially mechanical. They get blocked mostly in "extension" (i.e., fore and aft), and this in turn reverberates on the movement of the front limbs.

The main symptom of these lesions is a shortening of the stride of the front limbs. The horse goes out of his stall as if he were "walking on egg shells." He is "tied up, locked in his shoulders," all this being worsened by tightening the girth.

The reflexive contracture of the shoulder muscles releases somewhat while working, but the movements remain tight. The horse "pulls" on the reins and tries at times to snatch them out of the rider's hands, in an attempt to spread apart the spinal proceses of this area, which are "kissing"[6] and maintain the pain.

Another consequence of blocked withers is seen on jumping courses. Such horses rarely refuse to jump. If one prevents them from swerving off, they dash toward the jumps and never stop, even if it means jumping like a deer, without rounding their back. The blocking of vertebral ligaments prevents the lifting of the withers.

Their withers would hurt too much by stopping "smack" at the foot of the obstacle while in full gallop. Their courses are very fast and uncontrollable. They struggle to negotiate the combination jumps (in and outs), and they pull their riders' arms out of the sockets.

Blocked withers can be due to falls, [ill-fitting saddles][7] or even simply tripping up with the front legs. Such horses often stumble with one front leg repeatedly, which worsens their problem.

In the area of the withers, there are two particular syndromes:

The tenth thoracic vertebra is related to pulmonary conditions, especially chronic diseases like emphysema. Manipulating allows the horse to breathe somewhat better, but it nevertheless doesn't heal the patient.

The eighth and seventh thoracic are related to cardiac issues: when auscultation reveals a "click," manipulating the withers immediately releases this symptom.

T2 and T1, apart from the fact that their lesions may affect the nerves in the front legs, aren't linked to any specific pathology. The associated symptoms are the same as for the seventh cervical, but their intensity is usually less. On the other hand, their blocking is more stable and they are

---

6   Touching in the longitudinal plane parallel to the horse's withers—*Editor's note, Frances Williams M.D.*
7   *Editor's note, Frances Williams M.D.*

more difficult to manipulate. They cannot be easily reached by palpation, so the assessment of their lesion is difficult and requires some experience. Moving these vertebrae can only be done indirectly, by manipulating the cervical vertebrae whose adjustment is transmitted further back. This technique is only possible if all the cervical vertebrae are perfectly free. This maneuver requires the association of a lateral flexion, the ability to turn the entire neck.

Chapter 10

The cervical vertebrae

Like all other [normal] mammals, a horse has seven cervical vertebrae. The osteopathic lesions they present may have a traumatic origin (falls, wrong positions while rolling in a stall, medical injections incorrectly done...). But they are usually a compensation for a lumbar or thoracic lesion. They should not be overlooked during an osteopathic treatment. If one deals only with the blockings of the rear end a primary cervical lesion can be exacerbated.

The blocking of the seventh cervical is very frequent and associated with pathology of the entire shoulder and fore limb. Here again, horses show me every day that vertebral lesions may be the cause of troubles, as well as their consequences.

When C7 is in a state of lesion, the subject displays a brachio-cervical neuralgia (BCN in human medicine). The nerves in the arm, i.e., the brachial plexus, are irritated and inflamed by the local consequences of the vertebral blocking. There is pain and lameness induced from sensory fibers. There may be an alteration of the movement if the motor fibers are concerned. And there are practically always circulatory perturbances throughout the limb since the sympathetic fibers in charge of regulating the blood flux are in a state of imbalance.

When a horse displays a slight peritendinitis of the flexors, whereas the state of his tendons, slightly warm and soft, forebodes a tearing which, however, is still not present, one can practically affirm that his last cervical is blocked. A successful manipulation will take care of the troubles, before anything more serious happens. It, therefore, can be said that this vertebral lesion predisposes a tear.

Conversely, consider a horse with no blocking whatsoever at the level of his last cervical vertebra, who "clips" his front leg tendons with his rear toe; it is obvious that the tendinous lesion came first. If such a horse, however, is worked again with this traumatic lesion of the tendon, his C7 will become blocked in the course of riding!

This observation shows that regardless of the origin of the lesion, it is necessary to release the last cervical if one wants to effectively treat a sprained tendon. The circulation must be normal in order for the local treatments to work. This explains why so many horses have a pattern of repeated tendinitises: those are the ones who have kept a lesion at C7.

The blocking of the last cervical is not the only osteopathic lesion associated with a tendon sprain. There also may be a blocking of the pisiform (the bone which is above the tendon, behind the "knee" of the horse) and many other things to boot. I insisted on the connection "tendon-C7" because it is one of the most typical examples of the fact that a peripheral trouble may have a repercussion within the corresponding vertebra.

Many painful injuries of the front limb are linked to the blocking of the last cervical. A simple lameness due to too tight a shoe nail may bring up this lesion. The same applies to osteitis of the third phalange and navicular disease. In these afflictions, the vertebral blocking accelerates the harmful evolution by disturbing the circulation. I am sure that an old blocking of C7 may result in a navicular disease.

One more detail about the blocking of this vertebra: it is this very lesion which is responsible for the fact that a horse, lame in front, always bears his neck to the side opposite to the sore leg. A lesion in C7 does not allow him to easily turn his head toward the affected side.

C6 and C5 are only linked to mechanical phenomena, while partaking sometimes to a lesser extent than C7 in the irritation troubles of the brachial plexus.

C4 and C3 are involved with a serious affliction of the young horse: the "wobbler disease."

Wobbler disease occurs suddenly with some babies, aged 12 to 30 months. One finds the horse suddenly reeling and stumbling, mostly with the rear end, and this evolves sometimes up to a paralysis of the rear legs. Some cases stabilize their course on their own, but a healing is unusual, and most of these horses remain useless. An x-ray of the neck shows a narrowing of the medullary canal at the level of the C4-C3 joint. When the spinal cord is compressed, locomotion commands coming from the brain are perturbed along the course toward the muscles of the rear end.

The few positive results I've been able to observe subsequent to a manipulation of C4 have led me to set forth the following theory: some young horses are prone to getting the wobbler syndrome because they display a congenital malformation of the articular process of the body of the fourth cervical vertebra. This malformation, visible on an x-ray, is found at the level of the growth cartilage of the vertebral body. This explains why the affliction appears before two years of age. The sudden appearance of the symptoms is due to a fall or an accident which causes a blocking of C4 against C3, bringing the malformation closer to the medullary canal causing compression. The blocking is quite palpable and obvious and the manipulation is done easily.

Quite often, unfortunately even with manipulation, the symptoms don't regress, because some nerve fibers of the spinal cord have been destroyed by the compression.

There are, however, cases when the subject moves better and better in the following week and winds up being healed. These successes are only possible in horses whose nervous tissue was only compressed, but not destroyed.

I witnessed twelve cases of healing through manipulation; the most spectacular was that of a young horse who had been afflicted with the disease for three months to such an extent that he would lose his balance when one would clap the hands! He was clearly better three days after the manipulation and won recently in a local trotting race.

I believe that vets should try to systematically x-ray the necks of young horses of a bloodline where the risk exists. If one of them shows its articular process of C4 deformed, the accident will then possibly be avoided by refraining from turning the foal out in a pasture with other babies before the age of thirty months.

The second cervical vertebra (the "axis") is linked to very characteristic symptoms: when blocked at this level, such a horse refuses to "take the bit" as he works. He "drops the bit," moves his head sideways, is upset by the contact with the bit.

As it happens, C2 is associated with pain in the jaw muscles; indeed, the first muscular bundle to answer the action of the hand is the one which helps in shutting the mouth.

These symptoms I have just described can also be found with horses whose teeth ache, if the external edge of the upper molars is eroded, dental spurs hurt the cheeks. This should not come as a surprise: horses whose second cervical is blocked present a more irregular dental surface and need to be checked more often by the dentist than other horses. The pain in the jaw muscles causes uneven chewing and the wearing of the teeth is abnormal.

The atlas draws its name from Greek mythology since like the giant who was supposed to carry the earth on his shoulders, this is the vertebra which supports the head at the top of the vertebral column.

The osteopathic lesions one finds at this level are linked to all sorts of troubles affecting essentially the behavior of the horse. Apart from the local pain associated with the muscular spasm in the area, this blocking blocks arterial flow to the brain. The circulation is therefore asymetric, and the oxygenation of the brain is irregular.

The first consequence of such a lesion is well-known with humans, namely frequent and persistent headaches. No horse has ever complained of migraines, but when one has seen upon this very manipulation a depressed horse start playing again and neighing toward his friends in the field, and leave the corner of the stall where he would confine himself, one may conclude that it is not because they can't tell us that we should claim that animals never have headaches!

Circulatory troubles of the brain translate into perturbation of the organs of the senses, particularly vision. The horse then swerves and spooks frequently, as if he were afraid of the first leaf which moves in the wind.

I have seen many cases of aggressiveness, fear, depressive behavior bettered by the release of the atlas. But don't take me wrong, I'm not saying that all these troubles are always due to this lesion.

Chapter 11

Recapitulatory Chart

As concerns the locomotive troubles, this chart points out the *specifica*, but it is also understood that any blocking affects more or less the flexions, extensions, or lateral flexions of the horse as he works.

Vertebra	Locmotive Symptoms	Functional Troubles
Sacrum	various complaints on the hindend; hindend behind stiff, sciatica / femoral neuralgia	pneumo-vagina, paralysis of the rectum, vulva, penis; retention of the afterbirth
L6	sciatica or femoral neuralgia	Spasm of the neck of the bladder. Inflamation of the neck of the womb (cervix)
L5	sciatica or femoral neuralgia	?
L4	sciatica or femoral neuralgia	?
L3	sciatica or femoral neuralgia and patellar problems	Chronic diarrhea or smelly feces from perturbed flora.
L2	Sciatic or crural neuralgia, lubago of the galloper who engages too much.	Nephritis or renal in sufficienciency.
L1	Moves slightly sideways, "crooked."	Ovary troubles, testicle troubles, pain in a cord.
T18	"traversed" under the rider, stiff in the lumbar area	Stasis colic (constipation).
T17	"traversed" under the rider, stiff in the lumbar area	?(perturbation of adrenal glands).
T16	"traversed"	?

Vertebra	Locomotive Symptoms	Functional Troubles
T15	Rounds his back, "freezes" under the rider.	Excessive sweat. Second sweat in the stall.
T14	id.	Hepatic troubles. Generalized myositis.
T13	id.	Stomach, gastritis, yawning.
T12	id.	Diaphragm, distended belly.
T11	id.	id.
Withers (T10 to T3)	Stumbles "on the shoulders," gets out of the stall "walking on egg shells," pulls strongly on the reins	Respiratory discomfort, sometime cardiac troubles ("clank")
T2	id. C7	id. C7
T1	id. C7	id. C7
C7	Lameness in one shoulder. Cervivco-brachial neuralgia	One front leg is swollen. Peritendinitis.
C6	id. (lesser)	?
C5	id. (lesser)	?
C4	"Tilted" in his canter.	"Wobbler syndrome."
C3	id.	?
C2	Refuses the bit, shakes the head, chews sometimes with pain.	Dental spurs, Inflamation of the throat.
C1	Blocked in the poll.	Behavioral troubles, of the organs of senses.
Poll	Asymetrical movement of the rear legs; horse is difficult to ride.	Conduct disorders, sadness, aggressiveness.

Chapter 12

Balance of the hind legs

Before worrying about the type of work you will ask from your horse, make sure he is not in pain at rest!

Remember, the horse remains balanced on four legs not only in movement but usually also at rest.

Many horses get tired in a stall—box stall or tie stall. It is terrible to impose twenty-two to twenty-three hours of immobility a day on a horse who should move at will.

Some horses tire in a stall and even cannot sleep because of an overlooked detail which may seem trivial. This detail, i.e., the lack of heels in the hind feet, spawns a series of complex phenomena at the level of the skeleton. It is pointless to require any sustained work from a horse who has been unable to rest thoroughly during the night.

Everybody knows that a horse can sleep standing, and yet sleeping entails relaxation of all the muscles. A horse does not fall as he goes to sleep because his stifle and hock joints are attached to each other through a ligamentary system evoking the "*pantograph*" (this explains why one cannot extend the hock when the stifle is shut, and vice-versa).

In order to rest, a horse hooks his patella into a notch on the end of the femur, and in so doing locks his stifle and also his hock since both are interdependent. This mechanical locking by means of very powerful ligaments immobilizes the whole limb, and so the muscles may relax as the horse sleeps.

Horses susceptible to blocking their stifle (patella) are horses who display a relative shortening of the inside patellar ligaments and cannot liberate the patella from the position of rest.

As for the front limb, such a problem does not exist, since the "knee" (carpus) bends in the same direction as the ankle so that their alignment stabilizes them when in a resting position.

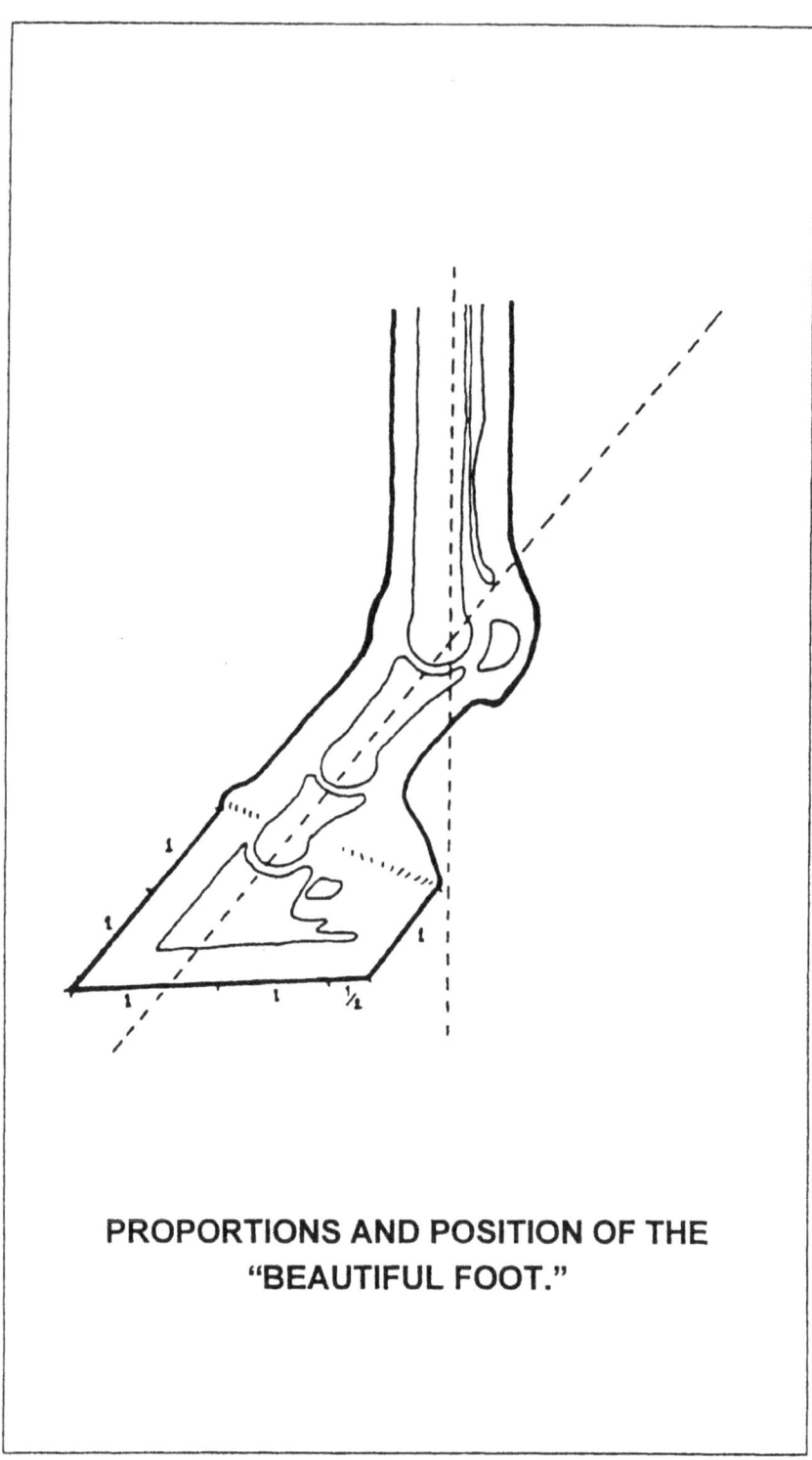

PROPORTIONS AND POSITION OF THE "BEAUTIFUL FOOT."

A horse cannot lean on a rear limb if his phalanges [fingers] are not in line. Seen from profile, his pastern and the front part of the hoof down to the toe must be perfectly aligned. Consequently, if a horse doesn't have high enough heels behind, he keeps his legs under himself in order to keep his phalanges in line.

Coming back then to the problem of resting, let us notice one, last important detail: a horse cannot hook his patella in order to rest if his cannon bone is not perfectly vertical (upright).

In order for the cannon bone to be vertical without losing the alignment of the phalanges, the hind foot has to have a high enough heel.

Horses whose hind heels are collapsed must keep the muscles of their back and croup tight, and one can often see them "sitting" against the manger or the stall door in order to find a support for relaxing. In stalls paved with cobbles, such horses always rest in the same spot because they found a cobble higher than the others, which allows their hind heels to be higher, thus facilitating a resting stance. (Moreover, cobbles have the advantage of keeping the foot and frog safe from humidity, which fosters the solidity of the heels. It is unfortunate that they have been abandoned to the current norm of concrete slabs which are resonant and much less wholesome!...)

To try to sleep, a horse deprived of heels has but one possibility: to constantly change his supporting hind leg. He locks one patella and tries to rest somehow on this limb while resisting the pain in his phalanges. When this pain becomes intolerable, he changes the supporting foot. One can imagine the quality of such a rest after twenty-three hours spent in this way!

Fatigue in the lumbar area added to the frequent changes of listing in the pelvis can suffice to spawn a blocking of the last lumbar vertebra and the withers, amongst others. If L6 is blocked, the horse urinates poorly and the hind legs swell, compounding his problems by increasing the discomfort.

Now, let's examine how to treat such problems. Your farrier will likely tell you that inserting wedges will make up for the lack of heels but compresses the heels and prevents them from growing naturally, and he is right.

After having tried several methods, I still think that wedges are a good solution. The treatments that allow growth of the heels, whatever they may

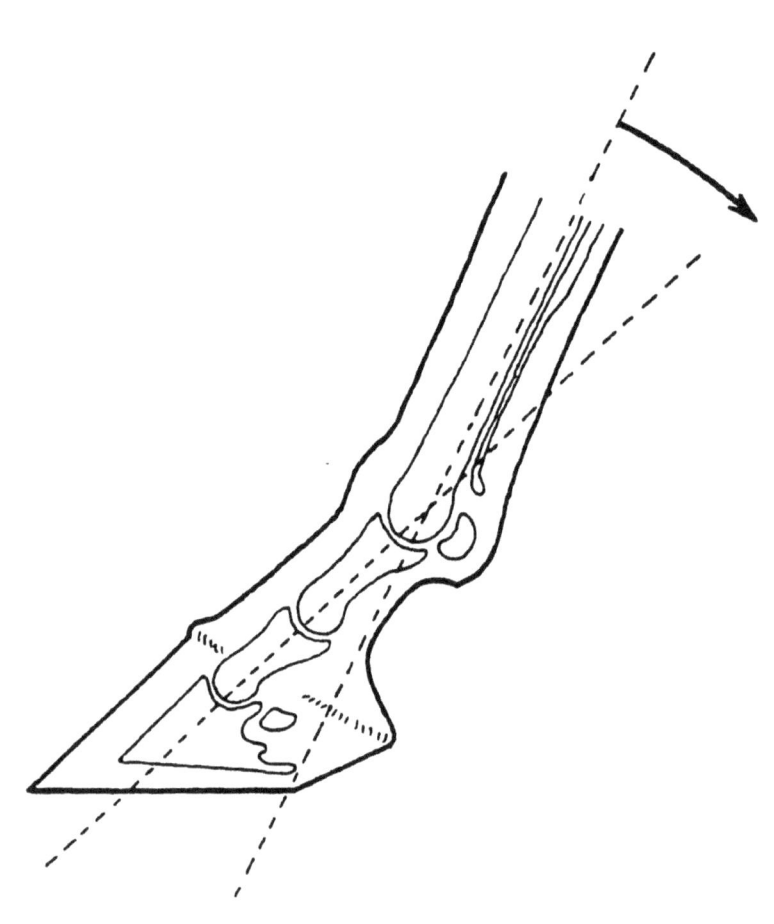

COLLAPSED REAR FOOT HEELS ⇒ SLANTED CANNON BONES ⇒ TIGHTENED BACK (PATELLA CAN'T PLAY ITS PART).

be, take some time before they work. I'd rather have the horse sleep better by the following night than to wait for a doubtful result while he remains in pain...

I am all the more convinced of what I'm saying as I was able to verify that the pain in the lumbar area and the blocking of L6 are often the origin of the absence of heels in the hind limbs. Even with wedges, or shoes thickened in the rear, the heels grow better when the horse's back is no longer sore. If this does not happen, it means that there still remains a cause for pain, in particular, likely a blocking of the sixth lumbar vertebra.

And even when one comes across a case when the wedges prevent the heels from growing, I still hold that the horse is better off being immediately rid of his pain than if he were waiting several months for hypothetical relief.

As soon as your horse has his phalanges and cannon bones in the correct position, you will observe the benefits in his work.

There are many horses who hurt more from spending twenty-three hours in the barn than from one hour a day of more or less good work.

Chapter 13

Balance of the front legs

Previously, I wrote that a horse cannot tolerate his phalanges not being perfectly aligned. This holds true for the four limbs. It is time now to explain why.

This statement is supported by two obvious reasons:

If the phalanges are in a state of hyperextension as is the case when the heels are low, the traction borne onto the flexor tendons becomes enormous. These tendons are inserted in the foot at the level of the third phalange and the small sesamoid, also named "navicular bone." It is well established that the inflammation of these bones creates a lot of pain.

The third phalange of the horse, which is inside the hoof, is very small and bears a considerable weight It is extended backwards by two points which settle in the heels of the hoof. These points, or "angles," are flush to the sole at the level of the "bars" and are not protected by the "digital cushion." In the case of slumped heels, they are traumatized and get inflamed by pressing on the sole and sometimes will even produce blemishes from within.

I explained how a horse avoids these inconveniences to the rear limbs by standing under himself, so as to keep his phalanges aligned. Unfortunately, he doesn't have the same opportunity with his front legs: the direction of bending of the "knee" doesn't allow him to bring his front legs forward enough in order to protect the bony structure of his feet. He therefore can't avoid the inflammation of the third phalange and navicular bone.

Finally, here is a very simple and fairly logical explanation of a fact that everybody has noticed: osteitis of the third phalange and navicular disease are specific to the front limbs although the physiology and mechanics of the foot are the same in front and behind.

In human medicine, "osteitis" usually refers to an infection of a bone. Equine medicine uses this word in its real etymological sense of "bone inflammation." Usually, when not specified otherwise, it just means "inflammation of the third phalange."

A horse with low heels in front lies down often and tends to waddle from one foot to the other. If only one foot is affected, he sets it constantly forward in order to relieve it. In the past, people would say: "he is showing the way to Saint James," after the name of the main slaughterhouse of Paris at the time.

Osteitis appears first in the front foot whose heel is more collapsed. Even if both feet are affected, lameness starts first with the collapsed heel.

Statistically, it is much more common in the left front foot.

Serious and in-depth statistical studies show evidence of a hereditary character for osteitis and navicular disease. Some bloodlines show a strong percentage, some don't.

But the reading of statistics may be misleading; osteitis and navicular diseases are not hereditary "per se." In my opinion, the transmitted factors in those bloodlines are very different. For some bloodlines, it is about a poor quality of the wall of the hoof, for others about a slight circulation deficiency with the whole skeleton and therefore these subjects react excessively to bone traumas.

A few years ago, I wrote an article that apart from a heredity of bloodlines, there could be a pseudo-heredity of breeding farms. Even if they are from different bloodlines, mares and babies of the same breeding are fed in the same way. If the minerals in the soil are not balanced, or if the animals are given too much of one mineral supplement, they will be more prone to having an aberrant bone-related reaction subsequent to a trauma.

I think that there is no heredity of bone-related problems with the horse's foot. There are bloodlines showing some vulnerability because they transmit slight blemishes which predispose to accidents which could have been easily avoided.

If I may allow myself such a crude comparison, what would one think of a researcher of humans showing that bruises and bumps are hereditary if this research had been conducted in families of near-sighted persons?

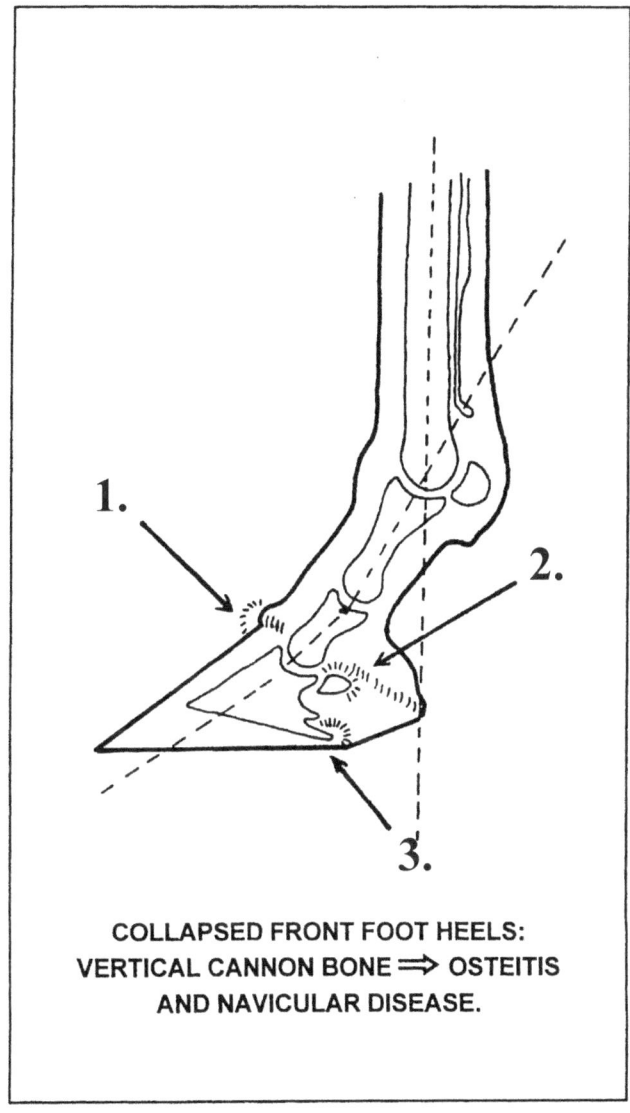

COLLAPSED FRONT FOOT HEELS:
VERTICAL CANNON BONE ⇒ OSTEITIS
AND NAVICULAR DISEASE.

1. Loading point in the area of corronary band
2. Heavily used insertion point of the deep flexor tendon
3. Broken by pressure of apophyses on the sole

With the condition of dropped heels, failure to load the distal forelimb: due to the fact that the horse must retain the vertical position of his tubular legs, he develops dangerous peak loads at certain fragile points.

As in the case of the hind hooves, one should not allow a horse to remain and cope with collapsed front foot heels. Act quickly, rather than waiting for months for the heels to grow. They may not.

Here again, wedges under the shoe remain an efficient tool, but they offer an important risk. The horse cannot list from one front leg to the other, thus he cannot protect his phalanges through changing position. Probably the time spent weight-bearing on misaligned phalanges has traumatized the "angles" and already started a still-undetected osteitis process. The wedges would then increase the pressure on those "angles" and then trigger the symptoms of osteitis.

Wedges do not create osteitis; they reveal visible symptoms of a lesion of osteitis which has already been in existence for some time, but had not yet manifested itself.

If lesions of osteitis are full-blown, the heels will be tender. Diagnosis can be confirmed by x-ray. "Swedish shoes"[8] allow the re-alignment of the phalanges, without compressing the heels, which gives these latter an additional chance to grow.

But caution! Swedish shoes are only helpful in particular cases. If the pain due to the collapse of the heels has propagated to the navicular bone through an excessive tension of the flexor tendons, such shoes will have disastrous effects, since they bear onto the frog, right under the navicular bone!

The "egg-bar shoe" bears up the heels whilst compressing them little and does not bear onto the navicular system. Anyway, each horse is a particular case, and it is the farrier's responsibility to judge the most appropriate shoeing.

Let us now answer this question of balance of the front legs from the viewpoint of osteopathy.

"Structure governs function," said Andrew Taylor Still. The lack of heels is sometimes due to a blocking of T2, T1, or more so C7. This lesion indeed sets the autonomic innervation of the concerned limb out of balance, while the autonomic fibers are in charge of regulating the blood flux in the vessels according to "Rule of the Artery."

---

8   (A shoe whose heels are truncated, but which comprises a trapezoidally shaped metal plate under the frog.—*Translator's note*)

One knows that with the human the blocking of C7 or T1 is accompanied by tingling in the fingers, from circulatory troubles. The same happens with the horse, as the horn of the hoof is ill-nourished; this hoof therefore grows slower and is weaker.

But let's not forget that the interaction between the vertebral level and the organ goes both ways. I have often seen cases of repeated blocking of C7 in horses with a collapsed front hoof. The solution then lies in elevating the posterior aspect by means of a shoe with thickened heels, or by a wedge to this foot.

Fitting a wedge to one foot only is very delicate. One should be sure of its necessity, since the result may be detrimental in some cases. With the human, more particularly the child, allopathic medicine has often wreaked havoc in this realm.

There are many people with one leg shorter than the other, but this occurs one of two ways.

The true short leg is rare. It is due to sequels of childhood illnesses or ill-repaired bone fractures. In this case, the shortening of a leg entails a tilting of the pelvis and a deformation of the vertebral column; it is then quite appropriate to rectify the length of the leg by means of an ad hoc pad, provided that the accident was recent enough so as not to have yet been compensated in the vertebral column.

However, the most common cause of an *apparently* short leg is a tilt in the pelvis. If in this case one sets a pad under the foot, one confirms the blocking of the pelvis which suppresses any possibility for a spontaneous release, and the compensating lesions in the spinal column are confirmed.

When a horse displays a collapsed heel only in one foot, we are dealing with a true shorter leg. It is therefore beneficial to compensate only this foot. However, in order to foster even shock absorption, it is perhaps advisable to put pads under both feet, while giving these pads a different thickness for reasons of symmetry.

I have seen horses whose blockings of the withers, the first thoracics, or the last cervical reoccurred constantly due to one collapsed front foot. This should not come as a surprise when one considers that with the human, walking twenty or thirty yards with a shoe whose heel is broken is enough to offset and block one side of the pelvis. This phenomenon is rarer with the horse's rear legs because the bones of this limb are set up like a "Z" so their height can be modified by the play of the muscles and tendons. The bony vectors of the front legs comprise an important vertical column so their height influences the balance of the whole.

Chapter 14

The saddle

The nervous system is distributed through the vertebral column which protects and supports it, as it supports the whole body in the course of the diverse movements of life.

It seems thence obvious that the division of the rider's weight should bear consequences on the general balance of the horse.

The mechanical balance of the horse has been studied at length by numerous equerries, resulting in all that has been written on the influence of "the seat" in horsemanship.

Health is another form of balance, and the first part of this book showed how much it can depend on the state of the vertebral column. The rider's weight, bearing on a column afflicted with lesions and therefore restricted in its movements, exerts an influence on the diverse pathologic troubles of the horse.

It is not rare to meet horses presenting the same trouble after each working session, whereas these very horses feel better as long as they are not ridden. I am thinking here of repeated "tying ups," but also of colic happening systematically after the working session, of horses which cannot urinate as they come into their stalls, of the many hepatic troubles which disappear after a few days of rest, etc.

Let us concentrate first on the influence of the rider's weight upon a sound column.

I have noticed on famous gallopers that the position of the saddle could influence the performance of the mounted horse. Particularly, several very good horses were presenting such a shape in their rib cage that the girth, hence the saddle, was naturally pulled back. Let's observe also that ponies mounted bareback by children display less cramped gaits than when they are saddled.

Finally, try to get some slack to the breast collar if by any chance you have to use one because the saddle tends to back up on your horse; let the saddle keep a somewhat posterior position, with respect to the usual one. You will notice that the horse is looser in his shoulders and that his gesture over the jumps or his gait extensions are better.

The explanation for this is simple when one knows the anatomy of a horse's vertebral column; seen from profile, the summit of the vault formed by the vertebral column lies where the horse's back is at its lowest point!

In architecture, the spot most apt to bear the weight in a vault is its summit (keystone). When the saddle is placed as forward as possible on the horse's back, it is assumed that the rider sits at the highest point, but in fact, due to the length of the vertical spines at the level of the withers, the rider's weight is applied in front of the keystone. This results in collapsing the front end, ever so slightly, and in pushing back the curvature of the vault. Remember then the expression "behind the bit." The horse makes you pass "in front" of him, and you do not get the lightness or the impulsion you wanted.

When the rider's weight is placed at the level of the ninth thoracic (this is not unusual), the back muscles are often tight, they withhold more than they hold in order not to collapse in front.

If the weight applies onto the twelfth or thirteenth thoracic (summit of the column), the back muscles have a lesser effort to exert, since the forces are better distributed between front and rear. A horse saddled in this way never stops all "stretched out;" his halts are perfect without one's needing to call him to order with the legs.

The diagrams added to this text show this system of keystone; they also make it clear that if the withers are slumped, if only so little, the long spines of the vertebrae in this area "kiss," inducing pain and a reflexive contraction of the muscles of the shoulders.

On the contrary, let's notice that if the rider's weight bears on the twelfth thoracic vertebra, the spaces between the spines of the withers open up, liberating the shoulders by the same token. The horse can then brace the muscles of his front end without having to tighten them in order to hold himself back. The gesture of his front legs becomes ampler and more efficient. Ridden in this way, a horse cannot "shift his rider in front of himself," he can engage his hind legs, and the whole movement is improved.

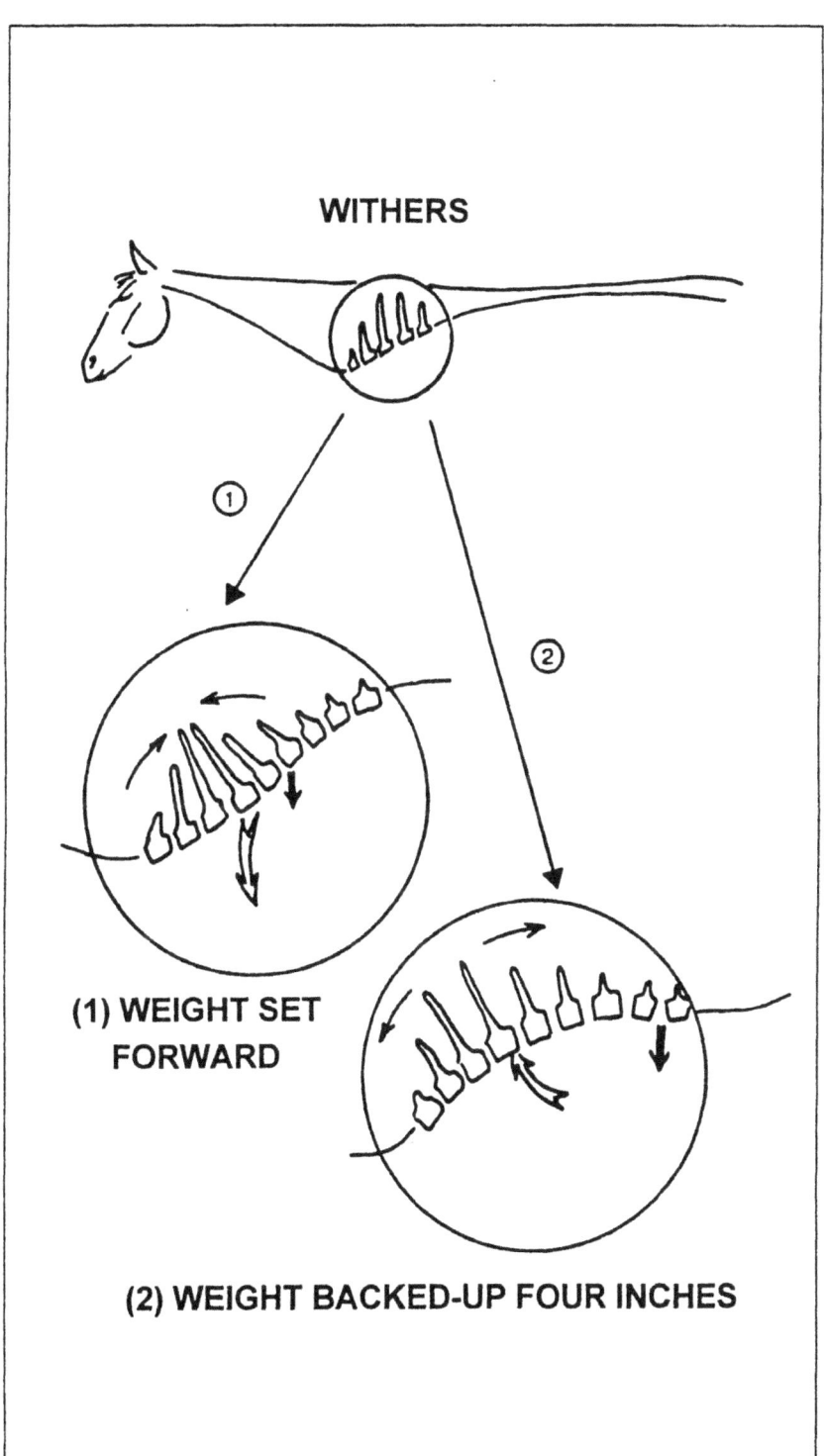

Due to their special conformation, some horses don't have to be saddled in this way, but the majority are better off if one takes this theory into account.

I'm not saying that one should sit toward the rear of the saddle; the weight is for the most distributed between the seat and the stirrup bars. It is indeed the whole saddle which has to be pushed back. I'm not saying one should change the rider's position (attitude), one should only change the spot of his seat on the horse's back.[9]

Some German trainers have understood this intuitively since they are usually working with a specifically shaped surcingle that they insert between the withers and the saddle.[10]

The first idea which comes to mind reading these lines is to wonder why all horses are not saddled in this way. It is because by backing up the saddle, one by the same token backs up the girth and the horse's respiration will be hampered by the pressure on the ribs this will create. The gallopers I have evoked in the beginning of this chapter had a sternum shaped in such a way that they would girth naturally farther from the elbows.

With most horses, one has to back up the saddle without backing the girth in order to get the advantages I have described. This would be possible by modifying the panels and the billets of the saddle, and this is already possible by using a special saddle blanket itself equipped with a girth, which maintains the saddle in a withdrawn position through an oblique girth which does not choke the horse.

---

9   (Dr. Giniaux is probably more exposed to jumping or all-purpose saddles, since open jumping is by far the most popular equestrian discipline in France. Dressage saddles do not place the rider's weight onto the ninth thoracic vertebra, since they present a "dip" much closer to the cantle than to the pommel. They place the rider's weight in the correct spot of the vertebral column. Unfortunately, their tree is designed in such a way that they bear on the horse's scapula, which creates all sorts of detrimental tensions in the area of the shoulders, and in the spinal column at the level T1, T2, T3, T4.—*Translator's note*)

10   (Fore girth—*Translator's note*)

Chapter 15

Working *downwards*, bending

It has often been said that working *downwards*[11] is beneficial for the back muscles. Yet some horses do not accept a normal head set after this type of work. Studying the vertebral column and its joints allows one to understand why.

To bring more light on this subject, I must start with some notions of anatomy.

The vertebrae are linked to one another by three points.

Two of them are the joints situated on each side of the vertebral arc through which the spinal cord runs.

The third point of fixation is the vertebral disk. It lies between the vertebral bodies, and is made of a gelatinous mass wrapped in a membrane which keeps it between the two vertebrae.

With the equine, this disk is of homogenous constitution as it does not comprise a harder central core as with the human's or the carnivore's.

This gelatinous disk is a shock absorber cushion between two vertebrae. The gelatin within it is not compressible; but the capsule in which it is wrapped is elastic.

The absorption of the movement between two vertebrae is therefore realized only through the capsule which limits the overflowing of the gelatin of the disk. The following diagrams show very well that if the vertebral bodies move apart, the diameter of the disk diminishes, whereas when they move closer, the capsule forms a roll which protrudes from the vertebral bodies. Therefore, it is obvious that we are in a better situation if the vertebral bodies do not come nearer to each other with respect to the resting position, since the mass of the disk would not find enough room and would force on the membrane, entailing a lateral protruding of the disk.

---

11 ("Long and low frame"—*Translator's note*)

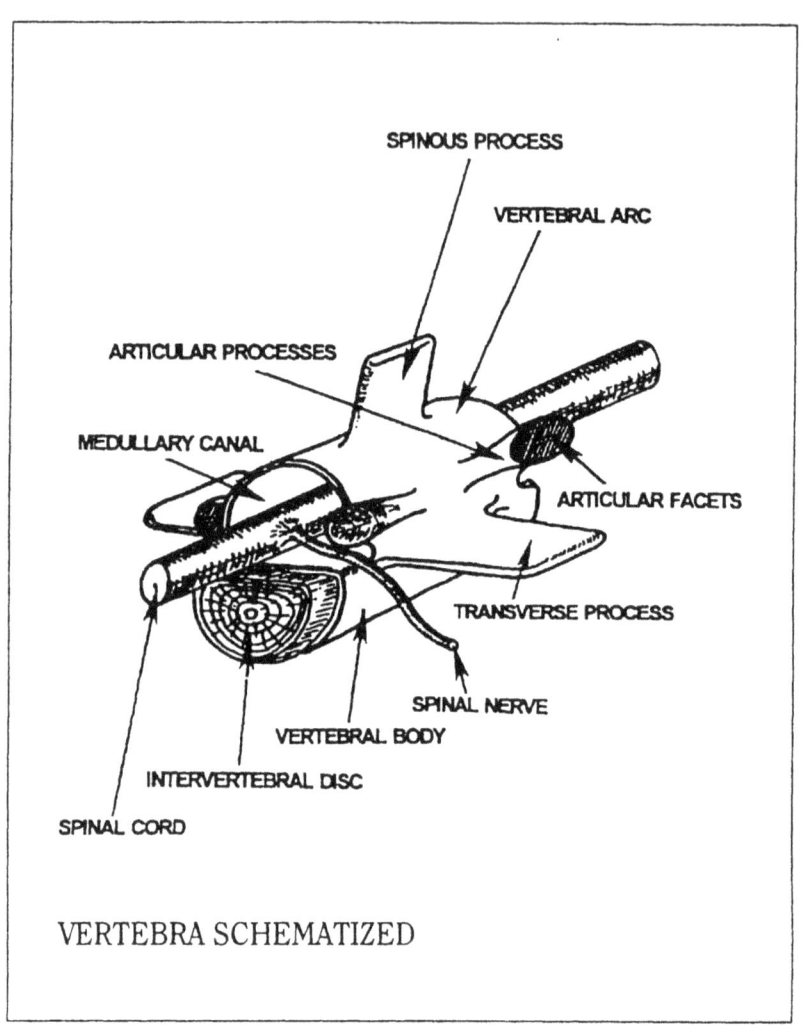

VERTEBRA SCHEMATIZED

If the famed "downward work" is done by bringing the vertebrae closer to one another, hence compressing the disks, those latter will form small hernias toward the medullary canal. The pain so created prevents a good musculation and provokes defensive reactions from the horse.

I said in the first part of this book that vertebral blockings are often due to a reaction of protection provoked by a painful movement; the blocking is meant to avoid the worse. If the position given the horse compresses one of the disks too much against the spinal cord, the two vertebrae concerned are bound by a spasm which, let alone being very painful, prevents an accident but prevents also any return to normalcy.

The horse, therefore, has a sore back and, in addition, he is incapable of bringing mechanically the concerned joint to a normal position as long as the lesion so induced has not been manipulated. He is in pain if one tries to lift his neck.

The same reason applies to a human, afflicted with a chronic lumbago, who cannot stand up from a chair if this chair does not support his lumbar vertebrae.

The pathology related to the horizontal plane also applies to lateral flexions. In osteopathy, one reserves the terms of flexion and extension to the movements done from front to rear (or more precisely, upward or downward for the quadruped). These terms will be more precisely explained in the following chapter, but let it be known for now that lateral flexions are what the riders call lateral bending.

Given the nature and behavior of the intervertebral disks, it is obvious that, as has always been stated by the Masters of horsemanship, any bending must be obtained by stretching the outside muscles, and never by shortening the inside.

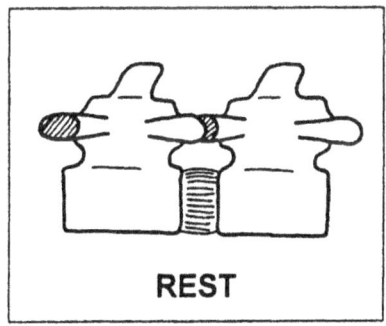
REST

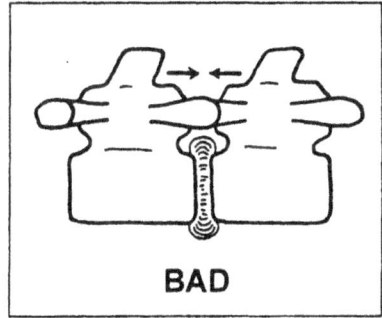
BAD

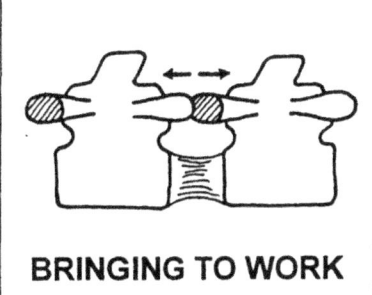
BRINGING TO WORK

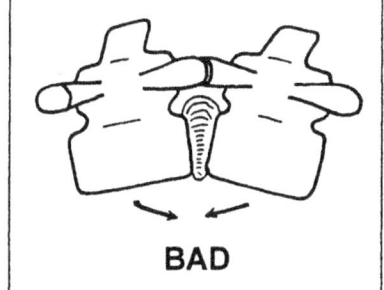
BAD

The same reasoning applies to the "shoulder-in" which, as anyone knows, must not slow the inside shoulder but advance the outside one.

One understands, therefore, the importance of the outside rein whose action induces the horse into stretching the outside, in the same way as, when lunging, an elastic rein on the outside will foster an extension of this side.[12]

Only an elastic rein, [a draped rein,] or a well-wielded running rein can act like the hand, to wit, keep a constant contact while following the movement of the stretching of the neck so induced (see foot note 12).

And since I am speaking of "tie-downs," I notice that it is too bad that the majority of them are hooked to the headstall, through the bit or not. Indeed, if the horse raises the head, a compression occurs between the occiput (skull) and the atlas. With the horse as with the human, a compression between these two bones is extremely painful. The horses, therefore, apprehend this kind of contact and are not willing to extend their neck; many of them "wince" on the contrary, compressing their cervical vertebrae to avoid pain. This works against the trainer's purpose, even if the position of the neck looks good.

---

12   (Translator's note: [Jean-Claude Racinet] takes strong exception to these statements. The outside rein should, in no way, induce inside bending; it should merely "accompany." To better judge the pointlessness of the usual literature on the outside rein as a bending tool, try the following experiment: completely undo one rein, the right for instance, from the buckle as well as from the ring of the snaffle, and, equipped only with the remaining rein (the left one), try to bend the horse to the right, with or without the help of the inside leg. It is impossible, and this shows that in bending the neck, the inside rein (which even Steinbrecht, the Master of the German School, calls the "bending rein") must be used first. Following this bending action of the inside rein, the outside rein should, on the contrary, yield. The neck will then bend harmoniously, since the yielding of the outside rein will provide amply for the necessary expansion. No compression on the spinal column can be waged in this way, for there is no traction in either rein; no traction from the inside rein, since the horse has yielded to it by bringing his head inward, and no traction on the outside rein, since it has yielded by the rider's own hand. Fostering the inside bending through an initial tension in the outside rein amounts to teaching a horse to pull. And he can become very adept at that.)—*Translator's note*

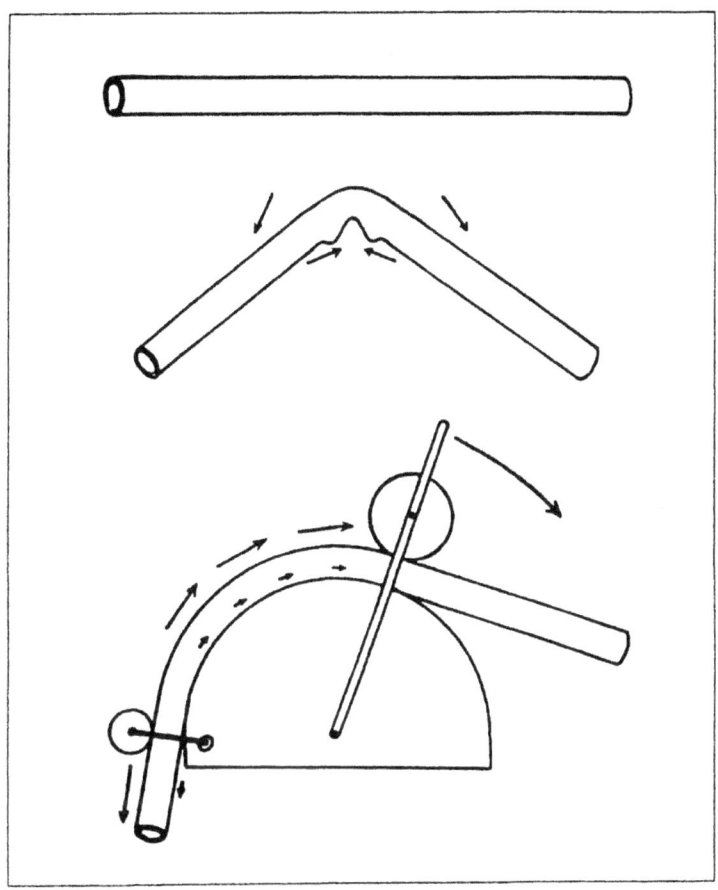

One would be better off using a "tie-down" which bears on the neck at the level of the second cervical vertebra; the horse then doesn't hesitate looking for a contact more toward the front by extending and "fanning out" his vertebrae.

To sum up correctly these notions of flexion and lateral bending, I will use an obvious and easy to remember image: when a plumber wants to curb a lead pipe, or a copper pipe, he doesn't content himself with simply bringing the two extremities of the pipe together by bending the inside side of the pipe, because this would drastically diminish the section of the tube. A pipe bent in this way would be damaged; its flow would be lessened. To correctly bend the pipe, one has to use a special tool called a "pipe bender" whose effect is to prevent the shortening of the inside of the curve and foster the extension of the outside.

One notices then that the inside is pulled as well, although much less than the outside. Bearing in mind that every movement should be done with impulsion, in the forward movement, these demonstrations confirm that, for a "shoulder-in," both shoulders must move forward, but the outside more than the inside. Ballet dancers and gymnasts who practice laterally flexed suppling movements know full well they must lift the outside shoulder and avoid collapsing the inside. The purpose here again is to extend the column so as not to compress the disks. To ask for an extension of the neck from the horse's back [when in the saddle], you may "comb the reins." You keep the contact as you follow the forward movement of the mouth [to promote elastic contact]. You can also use the same gesture as the ballet dancer: bring tension in one rein without blocking it, and follow with your hand the slight bending it provokes on the other side, avoiding any loss of contact; then act immediately in the same way with the other rein, and so on. Your horse's neck will then "undulate" laterally, entailing an extension of the whole of the spinal column. If, for lack of a good understanding of this process, you act alternately with your hands without yielding, the horse will lower the head, coming back onto himself or collapsing his withers; he will not extend the neck or stretch his back, and this will compress the intervertebral disks. A photograph taken in profile will perhaps be as pretty, but the horse will be in pain. Even if you don't know what a pipe bender is, bear in mind the following drawings with a pipe and the gesture of both hands when you bend your horse laterally or when you work from the lunge line.

The warm-up period, which must precede any sustained work in horsemanship, must have but one purpose: stretch the whole spine by "fanning out" all the vertebrae. Before contracting the big muscular masses, one must make room for the intervertebral disks in order to avoid any micro-hernia of the gelatinous tissue they are made of.

Now there exists a muscular system responsible for allowing the articular facets to slide apart. It is called the erector system of the column, and it is what humans set to work as they stand up, erect their torso, and try to grow taller; for the horse, it is solicited by slow and cadenced work, stretching the neck and back, while engaging the hind legs for the pelvis to pull back onto the column as the neck is pulling forward. One then can observe a lifting up of the withers and a "fanning out" of the spinal processes.

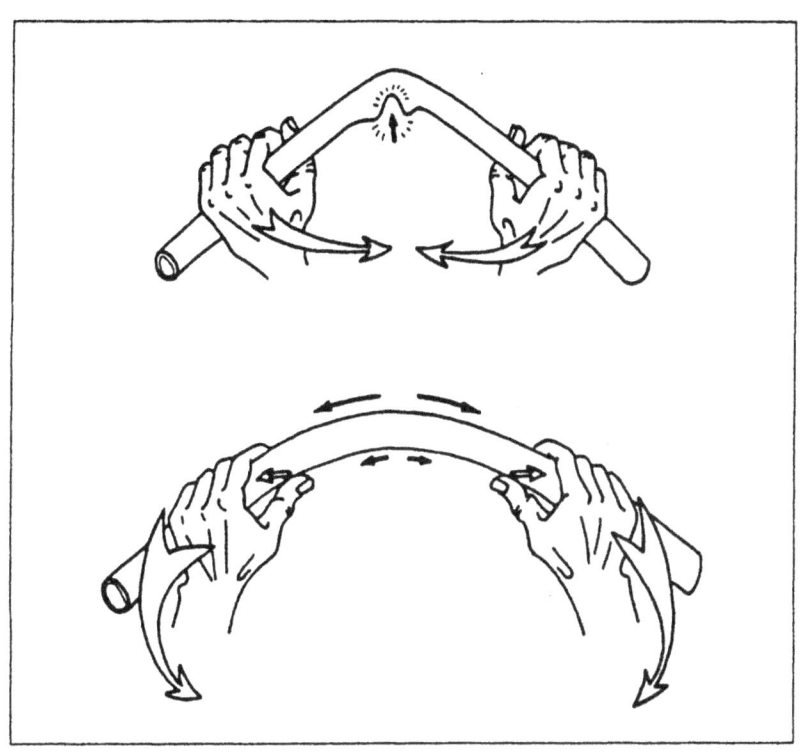

This should come as a prerequisite to prevent any ever so little "sustained" work from provoking pain or a reflexive blocking at some level of the spinal column.

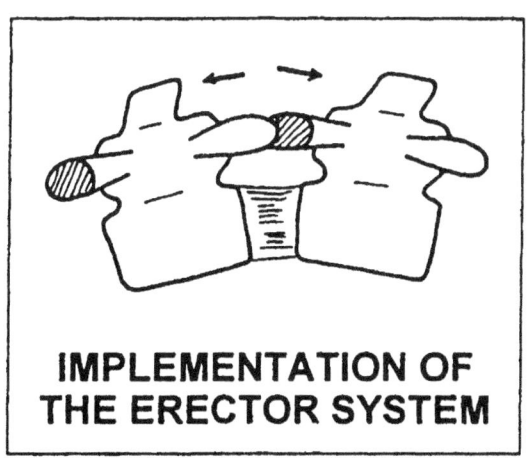

IMPLEMENTATION OF THE ERECTOR SYSTEM

Chapter 16

Correct Collection and elevation of the head and neck

All the riding masters insist on the necessity of a correct "collection" as a base for any work. The term is well chosen and fairly descriptive, as if a horse was made of several parts connected to one another. All these parts have to be put together so as to make sure we won't lose some while working.

A good collection results in engaging the hind legs, lifting up the back and more particularly the withers. Chapter 14 explained the importance of raising the withers rather than collapsing them, stressing the fact that the shoulders move more freely if the spinal processes of the first thoracic "fan out." Chapter 15 insisted on the necessity of stretching the spinal column before contracting the big muscular masses.

We have now to be more specific in describing the movements of the spinal column, in order to bring into light new and precise data about the process of bending.

Speaking of the movements of a segment of the vertebral column, we use the word "flexion" for the gesture which lessens the distance between the two extremities of this segment, and the word "extension" for the gesture which lengthens this distance.

Therefore, when looking at a horse in profile, the lifting of the back as the haunches lower corresponds to flexion of the thoracic and lumbar regions, whereas the lowering of the head is a stretching of the cervical (extension of the neck).

With the human seen in profile, the resting position displays a reversal of curvature of the lumbar segment with respect to the animals'. Rounding the back while tucking in the chin also entails stretching the cervical, flexion of the thoracic, and stretching the lumbar.

We are going to see that the curvatures displayed by the column in a vertical plane are necessary to allow lateral bending (lateral flexions).

Therefore, if your horse works with a flat back, you will get bendings of a lesser quality than if you flex his lumbar and thoracic. Hence you must lift the back and lower the haunches as he works. The problem of the cervical being more complex will be studied further on.

The vertebrae are linked by a tripod, one point of which is only a shock absorbing pad (the disk), the two others being the articular processes situated on each side of the axial vertical plane of the vertebral column. These joints allow trouble-free flexions and extensions, since these flexions and extensions are performed in this vertical plane.

Let's now imagine a column which, seen in profile, would be straight (rectilinear). The joints would still allow it to flex in this axial vertical plane.

But the lateral position of the joints (on each side of the vertical axial plane) would oppose any lateral flexion (lateral bending). This latter would be but very slight, within the limits of the sliding of the articular facets.

With all the mammals, the vertebral column offers natural curves in the median vertical plane, precisely to allow lateral bending of the trunk. This lateral flexion is then performed by fostering a rotation of the vertebrae around their longitudinal axis.

These explanations are rather complex, but try to grasp them well, since they lead to a cardinal demonstration concerning the bending of the neck.

In order to realize easily at home what happens in lateral flexion, cut out a band of cardboard about eight inches long by one inch wide, stick a tack in the middle, pointing up, and examine the following schemes:

Your cardboard band represents the surface in which the lateral joints of the vertebrae are, and the point of the tack represents a vertical process (spinous process) of this vertebral segment.

Keep first the cardboard band flat on the table and try to bend it laterally without allowing it to move away from the table. It is impossible and this shows one that lateral flexion cannot be obtained in the absence of vertical curves.

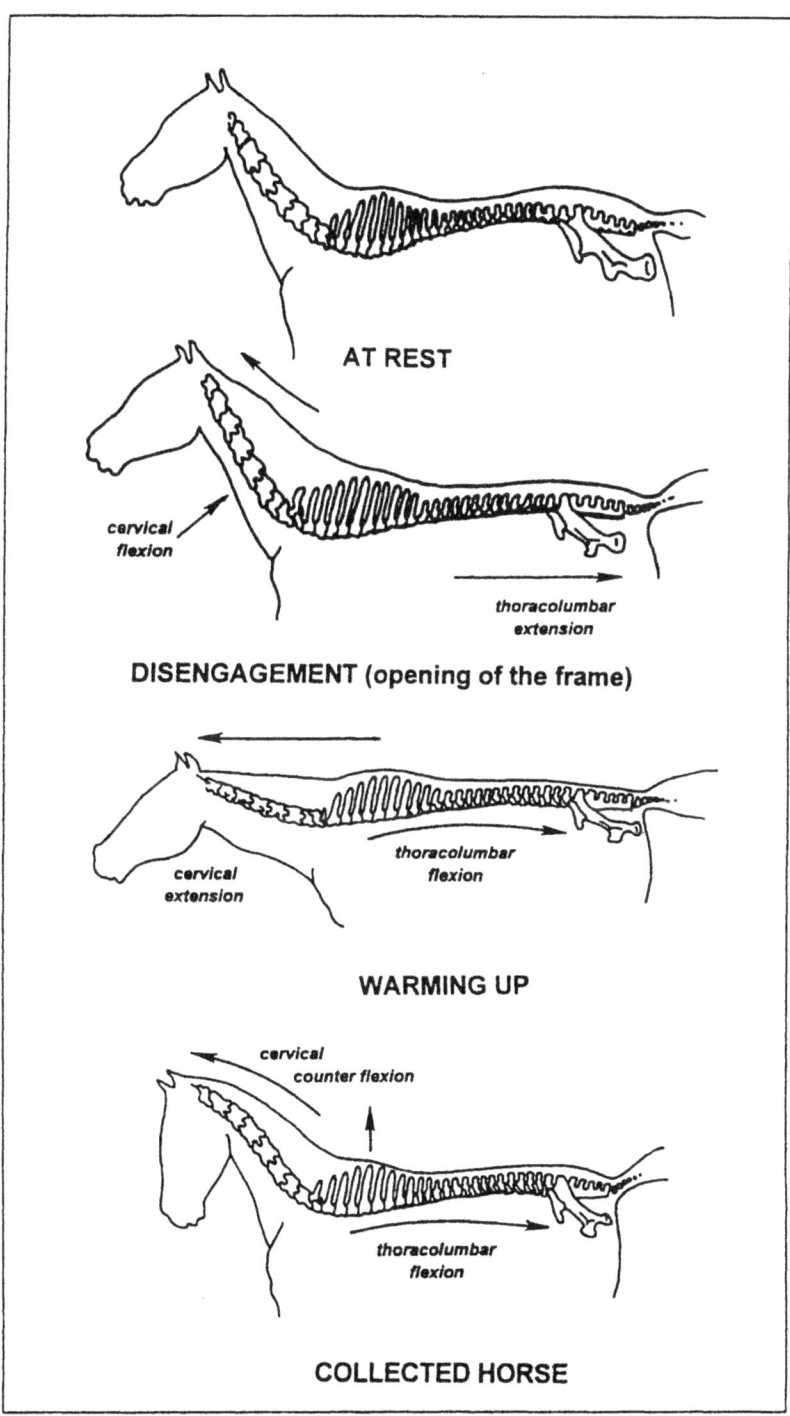

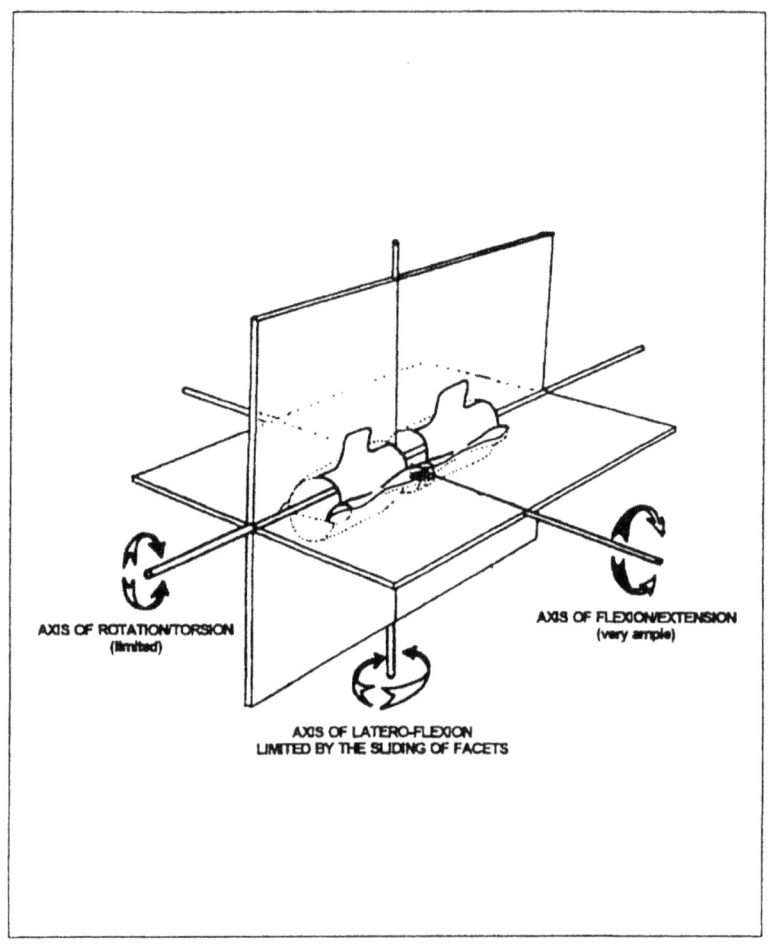

AXIS OF ROTATION/TORSION
(limited)

AXIS OF FLEXION/EXTENSION
(very ample)

AXIS OF LATERO-FLEXION
LIMITED BY THE SLIDING OF FACETS

If then you hold your cardboard band bent in a vertical plane, the tack being at the top of the curve, it becomes possible to bend it laterally, and you can see that the point of the tack rotates outward with respect to the flexion. If the band is bent the opposite way, with the tack in the dip, the same lateral flexion is always possible, but the point of the tack rotates inwards with respect to the flexion.

To conclude:

Those are indeed the natural curvatures of the column in a vertical plane which allow lateral bending.

If the back is round (convex), lateral bending entails an outward rotation of the spinous processes with respect to the bending.

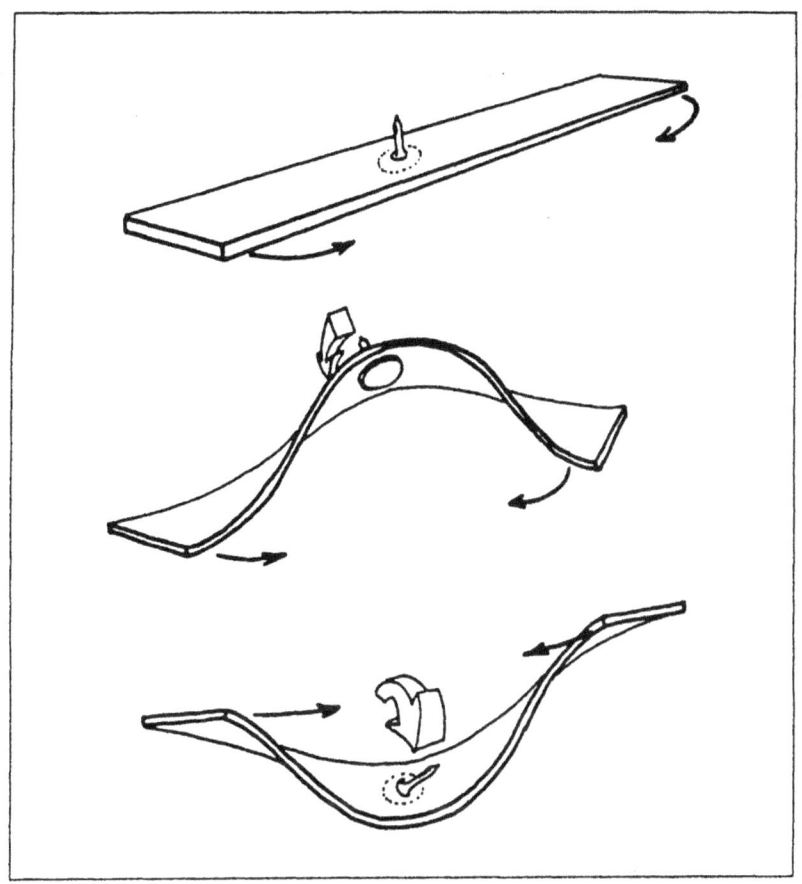

If the back is hollow (concave), a lateral bending entails an inward rotation of the spinous processes with respect to the bending.

If you have grasped these explanations, you now know why untrained horses who gallop at liberty bear their heads and necks outward when they turn:

If the thoracic and lumbar vertebrae are in a state of "kyphosis" (convexity), when the horse turns to the right his vertebrae rotate to the left. The cervical by contrast are naturally in a state of "lordosis" (concavity), and if he would bear his head and neck to the right as he turns to the right, his cervical vertebrae would rotate to the right.

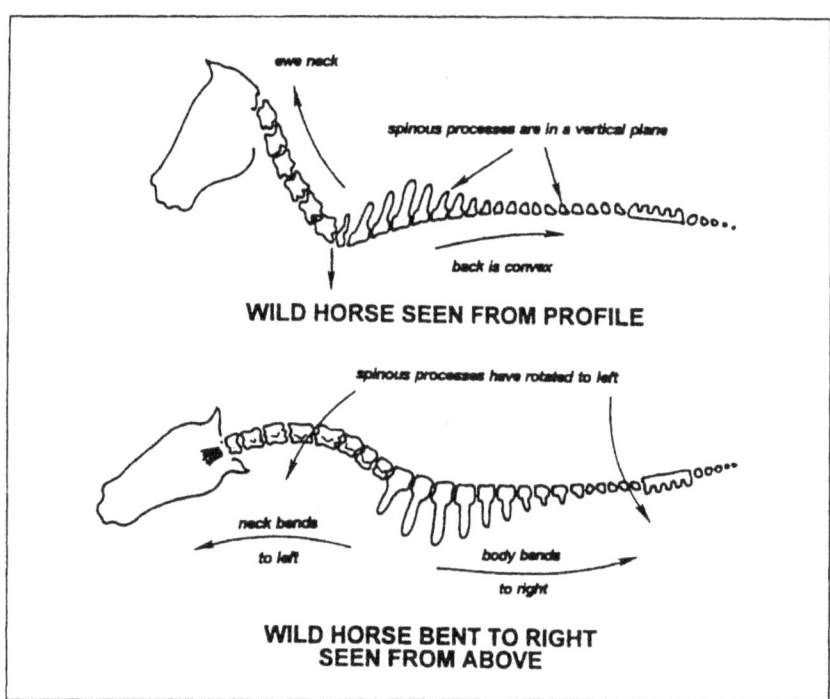
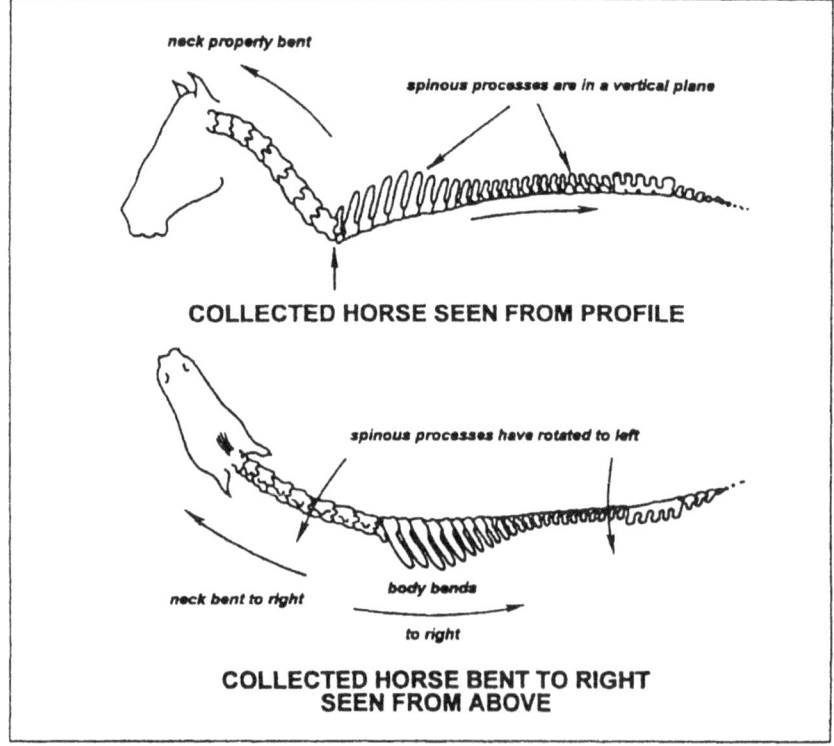

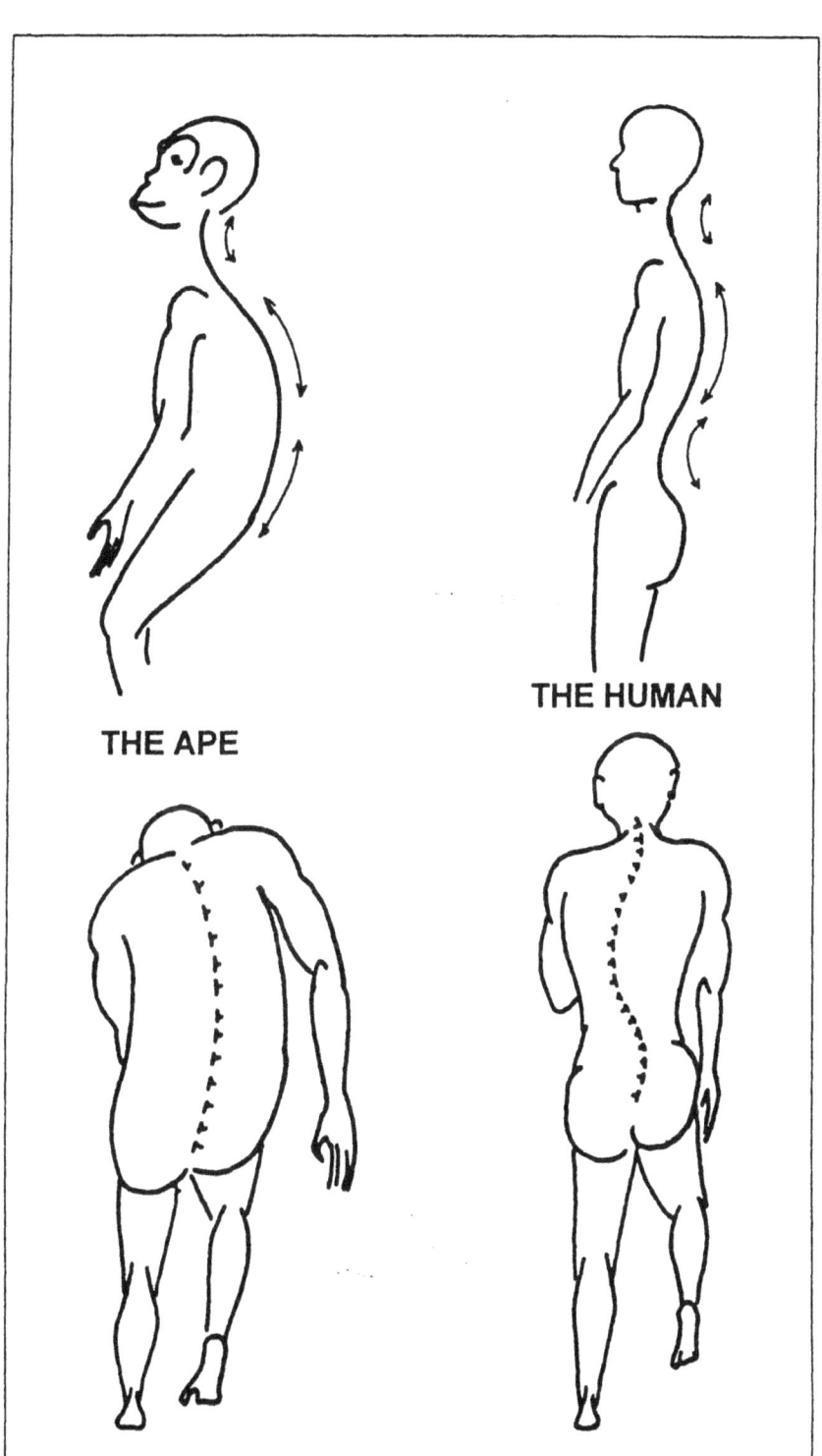

With spinous processes of the back tilted to the left, and those of the neck tilted to the right, guess what the spinal cord would undergo at the point of reversal of rotation!

What should be done to correctly bend a horse as he works, with the neck turned in the same direction as the volte he is tracing? We should reverse the position of the neck in a median plane, i.e., lift the base of the withers and foster a "yielding" of the poll while stretching the vertebral column so as to go beyond the alignment of the articular processes [shoulder].

The line of the cervical joints are then in a state of "kyphosis" like the thoracic and the lumbar, your horse can bend laterally from nose to tail without harming his column, all his vertebrae rotating in the same direction.[13]

The following diagrams explain in addition the difference between "leg-yeilds" one can ask from a young horse whose training is still in the beginning stage (head turned away from the bending) and the "half-passes" where the head must be turned toward the side of the bending, and which is possible only with a perfect neck flexion (withers uplifted and yielding at the poll).

The same rules about the rotation of the vertebrae apply to all mammals. Thus the human did reverse the curvature of his lumbar at rest (in profile) only to walk straight on his two legs without opposing the rotation of his lumbar and his thoracic. Their lateral bending is reversed with one another in order to walk without swinging the shoulders, but their rotation is identical. If an ape or a bear wanted to walk like a human by giving his column an "S" shape (seen from the back), the rotations of their lumbar and thoracic vertebrae would conflict and their spinal cord would be constantly traumatized by this torsion at the level between the last thoracic and the first lumbar.

---

13   (There still remains a "glitch" at the level of the junction between these two convex segments. It is difficult to believe that nature would allow two vertebrae, say C7 and T1, to display such diverging angles, to facilitate the all out convexity of the neck. And at the level C7-T1, there will always be concavity, including a rotation of these two vertebrae in the other direction. So it seems that these two vertebrae are solicited by conflicting forces anyway. (Dr. Giniaux agreed on this later and tuned up his analysis [see Appendix 1].)—*Translator's note.*)

Chapter 17

What to do when facing a problem

The preceding chapters described the complex movements of the vertebrae of a healthy horse, but an articular blocking may often disturb and further complicate these movements.

Let us examine some types of lesions, and the proper way to solve them while working the horse.

Imagine a perfect horse, offering no flexion-extension troubles or latero-flexion difficulty. You work him daily, but one day, you feel a reaction of defense against the lateral bending on one side. He probably rolled and got cast in his stall during the night, or he made a wrong movement which blocked the vertebra whose system of support was weakened by an oncoming affliction (ovary trouble for LI, kidney congestion for L2, etc.).

Let us for instance consider a blocking of T15 preventing a correct bending to right; schematically, his vertebral column looks like this:

The three vertebrae indicated in the circle are blocked together in this position, and it is visible that a bending to the left is possible, whereas the lesion opposes a bending right.

What I explained in the previous chapter shows that the spinous process of T15 is offset to the right. Indeed, the natural kyphosis of the thoracic vertebrae induces an outward rotation of this spinous process in case of a lesion bringing a state of latero-flexion to the left.

This detail allows the osteopath who palpates him in his stall to affirm that your horse cannot bend to the right, since he feels a spinous process blocked and offset to the right with respect to the alignment of the other spinous processes.

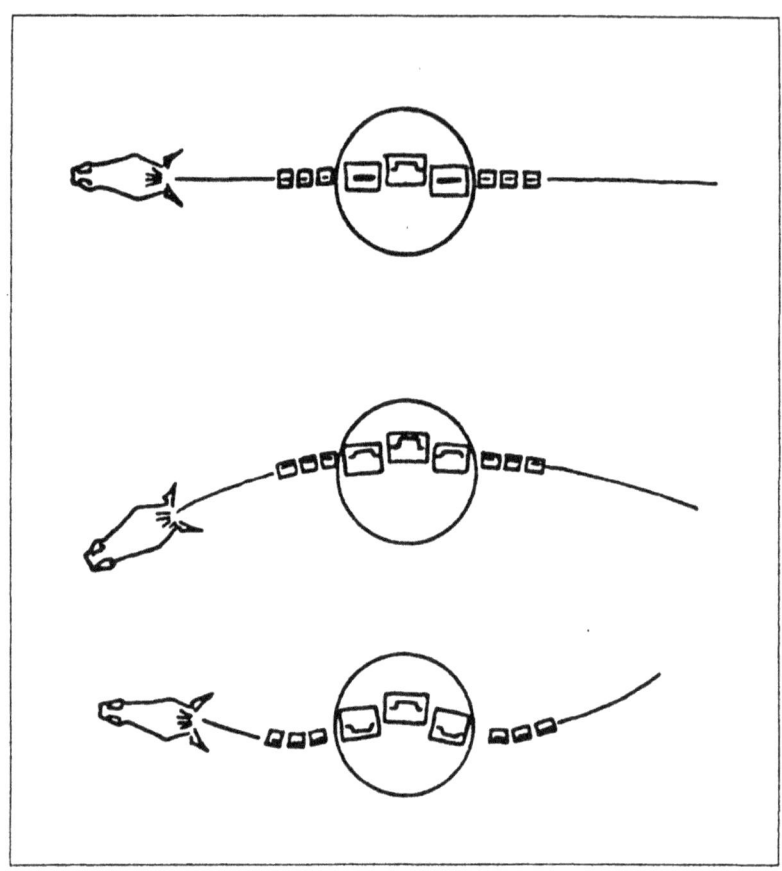

It is this feeling of displacement of the tip of the spinous process which is the origin of the famed expression "displaced vertebra" which has been so harmful to osteopathy when physicians or veterinarians hear it from their clients' mouths.

Let us come back to your horse who has but one lesion, and yet fights as you start a right bending; your attitude in this instant will bear a capital importance:

(1) If, as it happens sometimes, you insist in bending him to the right with the firm intent to make him yield, the diagram shows that you will markedly increase the pain at the level of the disk situated between T14 and T15. But, and above all, if you end up getting the desired right bending by force, you will have in fact worsened the lesion and the original spasm: you will have provoked another blocking which compensates for the first one mechanically!

This new lesion happens sometimes just ahead of the first one (T14 in this case), and you feel then that the horse is mechanically improved, but the lesion at the level of the disk strained by two opposite blockings is so serious that the animal starts an important myositis. He is in a big autonomic trouble corresponding to the level of the lesion. For the case we are dealing with, it will bring about excessive sweats with additional sweating in the stall, and a hepatic dysfunction which will reflect on the whole state of health of the horse.

More frequently, the compensating lesion will come up at the level of a cervical, and the horse will seem to be better because he will make up for the lack of bending to the right through an exaggerated latero-flexion of the neck. However, this new blocking will make him tip the head to the right when you ask for a volte to the left.

One may even go further in this example and imagine that the compensation came up precisely at C6 or C7. The horse then finds himself afflicted with a cervico-brachial neuralgia concerning a shoulder, followed with circulatory troubles with this limb and a tendinous problem or even osteitis if the blocking lasts long enough to entail a malnutrition of the phalanges and subsequent ossification troubles (it may take only a few months).

The side concerned with these perturbations will depend on the direction of the curvature of the neck at the moment when you got the bending to the right by force, since the direction of rotation of the cervicals depends on the position of the neck in a vertical plane.

(2) Bearing in mind the image I gave you at the beginning of this book as I was introducing a comparison with the "ratchet" of the hand brake of a car, you will sometimes be able to release the blocking by the first strides of your horse if the lesion of T15 is not yet compensated.

Observing that the bending to the right is mechanically difficult whereas it was easy the day before, make one or several voltes to the left, smaller and smaller in a spiral.

As you went out of the stall, you assessed the level of the vertebral column where the resistance to bending is felt and you just have to ask for the maximum left bending at this level (right behind your left leg in the case we are dealing with here).[14]

If the problem lies at the level of the cervical vertebrae, you know now that the position of the neck does matter, but a long reasoning is not necessary to find the solution: ask your horse, he will show you. The release is at the end of the only movement mechanically possible: flex the neck on the easy side, and you will feel if it is easier with the head in a high or low position.

With respect to this, I have here to stress a point which matters to me much; some osteopaths hold that the manipulation should be done in the direction of lesser pain yet the horses contradict them rather often. For me, the manipulation has to be done in the mechanically possible direction; there are indeed cases when the lateral flexion is impossible, but not painful, while the opposite movement is possible, although painful. This pain may be mild, but it is still stronger than in the other direction where it is nonexistent. It is about cases where the spasm is such that it is impossible to force upon the lesion and modify its features on the mechanically resisting side.

What I just explained for the problems of bending holds true for the flexion and extension of the back or neck and for many other things in horsemanship.

If you cannot solve a problem in this way, it means that your horse presents already several lesions which compensate each other. In this case it is necessary to come up with more precise manipulations which cannot be done from horseback.

The study of the movements from an osteopathic point of view allowed me to explain in a logical way what some great masters of horsemanship always practiced instinctively; I content myself with confirming their teaching to the extent where a well-understood reasoning may induce you all the more to follow them.[15]

---

14   (It is more advisable to look for the bending using only the hand and seat. The use of the inside leg may introduce a contradiction, as it tends to foster an inward rotation of the rib cage (see Appendix 1).—*Translator*.) [The opinion in the note above is that of Jean-Claude Racinet.—*Editor's note*.]

15   (As a matter of fact, Dr. Giniaux's discoveries also allow us to challenge the equestrian lore, when necessary. (See Appendix 1)—*Translator*)

Chapter 18

The manipulations

It is deliberately that I don't give details on the techniques of manipulation of a horse, this for several reasons:

A person who would be capable of practicing only one or two manipulations would be dangerous for the horses he/she would be entrusted with. As I have said several times in this book, a patient amenable to a treatment by manipulations has rarely only one lesion. The very fact of living and moving with this lesion will rapidly have set off others by compensation. It would be wrong and sometimes even dangerous to overlook some of these lesions, while the acquired "wrong balance" of the organism is modified.

Knowing how to manipulate a horse is one thing; knowing what to manipulate and in which order and direction is another.

The matter is not to flex everything in every direction hoping that one of these movements will be beneficial. One must foremost compel oneself to fine tune one's "touch" to attain the finesse of palpation required for diagnostic accuracy. This manual language I have spoken of in the beginning of this book is not only difficult to acquire. But like any foreign language, it will be lost if not frequently exercised. Its full use, as the mastery of its complexities, requires daily practice.

- While a pattern of a manipulation can be described in its main features, its achievement depends on each individual case. In particular, the precise timing of the intervention in the course of the bringing into position cannot be described, it can only be "felt."

So besides knowing the techniques and being able to feel the lesion, one also has to feel the instant when the whole structural environment of this lesion is favorable to the achievement of the act itself. Acquiring this feeling takes much time.

There are lesions not to manipulate in some pathological contexts, particularly if the internal functional trouble they compensate were to be too serious for the patient. One therefore must have an in-depth knowledge of equine pathology to avoid treating some diseases which would be more amenable to other therapies and which, by contrast, would be worsened by this method.

Finally, and this sums it all up, I mention that osteopathy does not consist of manipulating. It is a way to *assess* the balance of an individual and diagnose his/her troubles. Palpation is its approach and language. It is through the hands that it also reaches its ends, but this is the final stage.

Knowing how to manipulate does not make one an osteopath!

On the other hand, since the horses are trained as high level athletes, it is undeniable that more and more equine osteopaths will be needed. This can be attained only through a comprehensive education and exams to sanction competence. The proliferation of people blindly manipulating, unaware of the consequences, could only be harmful to the horses and detrimental to the reputation of the method.

Conclusion

I see new horizons constantly opening, but I can write them down only to the extent that I have verified new theories.

The knowledge of the joints in the limbs and their relation with internal troubles is full of promises. For instance, I have been able to notice several times that the tendinitis of the flexors is accompanied with a blocking of the "pisiform." This little bone, situated behind the horse's "knee" (the wrist in the human) plays a capital role, since it works as a "fulcrum-pulley." The blocking of this bone disturbs the transmission of the muscle contraction to the tendon which is then left alone to take in charge the shock absorption as the foot sets down. This could explain some cases of repeated tendinitis, all the more as the release of the blocking of the pisiform through a manipulation results in a rapid healing of the tendon.

The tendons, ligaments, the muscles, and even the internal organs have their say in osteopathy, and this exploration is only in its initial stage.

I hope that this work will have helped you in understanding what the osteopathic concept is, and that osteopathy will allow you to better understand the behavior of the horse as he works.

The basis for equine osteopathy being established, its development will grow more and more rapidly. I am convinced that in a few years from now, it will not be conceivable anymore to train a horse without monitoring him from this point of view. The same as the "comprehensive profile" of the blood and the cardiac recuperation ability of an athlete under training are constantly checked, so should his structural features.

Osteopathy plays a part in the afflictions of the locomotive apparatus, nobody would deny it. It has its say in the chronic diseases, as you have learnt from this book. Let it be known finally that it is very useful in the prevention of acute diseases.

The race horses I am following are much more consistent in their performances because they undergo a lesser amount of unexpected interruptions in their training programs.

A last detail remains to be mentioned: if you present the osteopath with a bad horse in pain, he will make out of it a bad horse in less pain. I mean to say that osteopathy can restore the balance of the individual, but cannot turn a plain horse into a star. A horse in good health is not obligatorily a champion.

APPENDIX 1

Dura Lex, Sed Lex (hard law, yet law)

In 1929, the year I was born—great events never come alone—Albert Einstein provoked some commotion with his theory of relativity, because of the enormity of the changes it implied for our conception of the universe.

Hard to believe, at first, that the universe is *curved (!)*, that time and space are relative to each other, that whoever would travel at a speed greater than that of light would go back in time, etc. And still, this theory is justified every day, as science progresses.

So Dr. Giniaux, of France, must be some kind of a little Einstein in his field, because he also came up with a new law which is likely to force us to consider horsemanship and the horse in a new light.

This law concerns the bending of a horse's spinal column. It states that if a horse bends laterally without in the meantime rotating the line of his spines, the bending will be very limited; but if the spines (i.e., the vertical processes of the vertebrae) rotate around the longitudinal axis of the spinal column, then the possibilities of lateral bending are greatly increased.

And here comes the important point; if this rotation is done *outwards* with respect to the lateral bending, the spinal column will take a *convex* (round) profile, whereas if the rotation is done *inwards* with respect to the lateral bending, the spinal column will take a *concave* (hollow) profile.

To make all of this more intelligible, I reproduce hereunder, and with his permission, the drawings of Dr. Giniaux's book *Les Chcvaux m'ont dit* (*What the Horses Have Told Me*). Imagine the horse's spinal column as a cardboard band; it cannot bend laterally. Now pin a tack, facing up, in this cardboard band, to represent the spines, or vertical processes, of the vertebrae. A lateral bending becomes possible if the cardboard band is given a "convex" profile, which brings about an outwards rotation of the tack; the same lateral bending is also possible if the cardboard band is given a "concave" profile, entailing an inward rotation of the tack (see page 99).

The three characteristics (lateral bending/outward rotation/convexity or lateral bending/inward rotation/concavity) are inseparable. If you have two of those items, you obligatorily have the third. For instance, if you have convexity and a rotation of the spine, you will create a lateral bending opposite to the direction of rotation. If you have lateral bending and convexity, you will create an outward rotation, and if you have lateral bending and outward rotation, you will create convexity. And the like for the inward rotation vs. concavity.

This law can hardly be challenged, since it has served as a basis for the thousands, or tens of thousands, or perhaps hundred of thousands, of osteopathic manipulations performed successfully by Dr. Giniaux, his students, and his followers since it was established.

Let's now examine the consequences of this as concerns the schooling of a horse.

Take the circle, for instance. In *The Gymnasium of the Horse* [Xenophon Press, 1994], the German author, Gustav Steinbrecht (1808-1885) states that when working on a circle, the horse's inside hind leg is over-loaded with respect to the outside; but in at least two footnotes, Col. von Heidebreck, who edited the 1935 edition, objects that no, no, with all due respect due an old master, Steinbrecht is wrong, it is the outside hind leg which is overloaded.

Well, Col. von Heidebreck's intuition was right, since when a horse is bent to right for instance, his right hip is *lifted* by virtue of the outward rotation of his spinal column (Fig. 1). If the inside hip were lowered instead, then there would be an inward rotation of the spine, and the horse's back would be hollowed, which is certainly not the purpose of working on a circle.

This lifting of the inside hip certainly puts more stress onto the outside hock which is then obliged to *bend* however much to restore the evenness in the actual length of the rear limbs of the horse so as to assure the regularity of the gait.

This slight bending of his outside hock (as the outside hind foot is still on the ground), and it only, will allow the horse to set his inside hind foot down on the ground while proceeding forward on the circle in a bent position. All the interest of the work on a circle lies in this beginning of suppling of a hock, the outside one as it happens. This advantage is further enhanced in a shoulder-in. I am here referring to the exercise as understood by its creator, La Guérinière, in which the movement is lateral at the level of the haunches as well (meaning that the hind hooves set down *aslant* with respect to the direction of march), entailing a setting down of the inside hind foot in front of, that is, *in the axis* of the outside hind foot. Since it has a lateral component, this movement of the inside hind leg is more difficult than when going forward on a circle and will require an increased bending of the outside hock, which is the main advantage of this exercise.

One will notice that so far, and since it was described for the first time in Chapter XI of *Ecole de Cavalerie* [Xenophon Press, 1992], the idea was that the right shoulder-in would lower

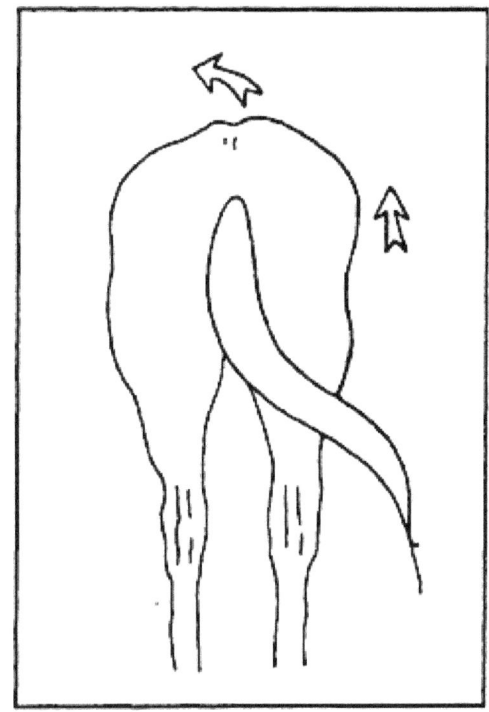

Fig. 1 - Horse bent to the right.

the right hip and thus work the right hock. Well, that was apparently an error, but the adjustment we have to accept here is of little importance and does not deny the usefulness of the exercise.

Let's come back, for instance, to our circle. We have always been told that in any bent movement, the line of the horse's ears should remain strictly horizontal. Why?

Probably first for cosmetic reasons, but also because we want to bend the horse *our way* and not his. When a horse yields more with his nose than with the top of his head, we think that he is resisting, whereas in fact he is thoroughly yielding *his way,* because a horse *has to* rotate the line of his spines if we want him to bend fully. Now, if we keep the line of his ears horizontal, we keep the spines upright by the same token. So the horse will bend in his neck, which is more supple. But his body will display only the limited bending it can give in the absence of any rotation of the vertebrae.

Becoming aware of this allowed me to conceive a little trick to keep my horses on the bit when they tend to stiffen at their poll. I just pull the nose

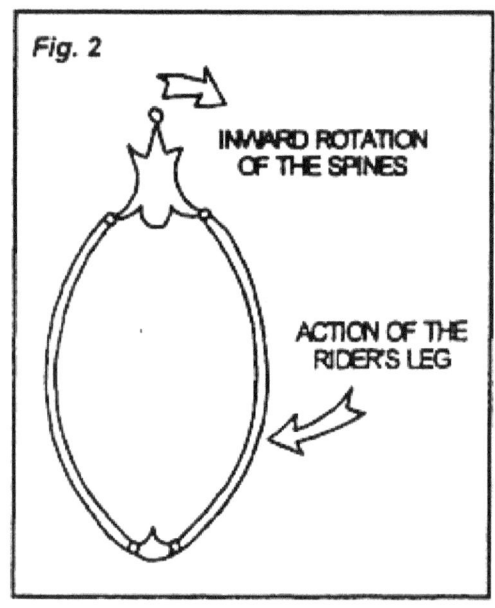

Fig. 2
INWARD ROTATION OF THE SPINES
ACTION OF THE RIDER'S LEG

(and only the nose) inside, so as to make the first vertebra, the atlas, rotate outwards. The other vertebrae are very likely to follow suit, if only because of the law of lesser effort, so the horse bends laterally, raises his back, and goes back onto his bit. Try it and keep me posted.

Another very unexpected consequence of Dr. Giniaux's law is that when a horse is bent laterally, his rib cage will bulge *inwards* (as an effect of the outward rotation of its vertical axis). Now this is a good one, because it positively invalidates the common belief that a horse should be bent round the rider's inside leg!

If our inside leg were strong enough (but thank God, it is not!) to push the ribs outwards, then the withers would tilt *inward*, entailing a *hollowing* of the back (Fig.2)!

I have always felt queasy with the story that a horse should be bent through the pressure of the rider's inside leg. And God knows we were bombarded with this from all quarters, German horsemanship as well as French, not to forget the good General L'Hotte, the Messiah of Saumur. Not that I had had in the least any intuitive knowledge of Dr. Giniaux's law to come, but for me it stood to reason that there was no common measure between the strength of my leg and the rigidity of an equine rib cage. Besides, how tiring! How boring! Force your horse! Sweat! Ugh!

So, what happens when we use our inside leg in the fallacious hope of bending the horse? Positively nothing. We fatigue the horse and our leg by the same token. Thank you, Dr. Giniaux. Now if I am right, why have we not found out earlier about the lifting of the inside hip and the inward bulging of the rib cage? Anthropomorphism! We build in our mind an imaginary horse who acts like a little man on all fours, and we reason our horsemanship from this horse, not the real one.

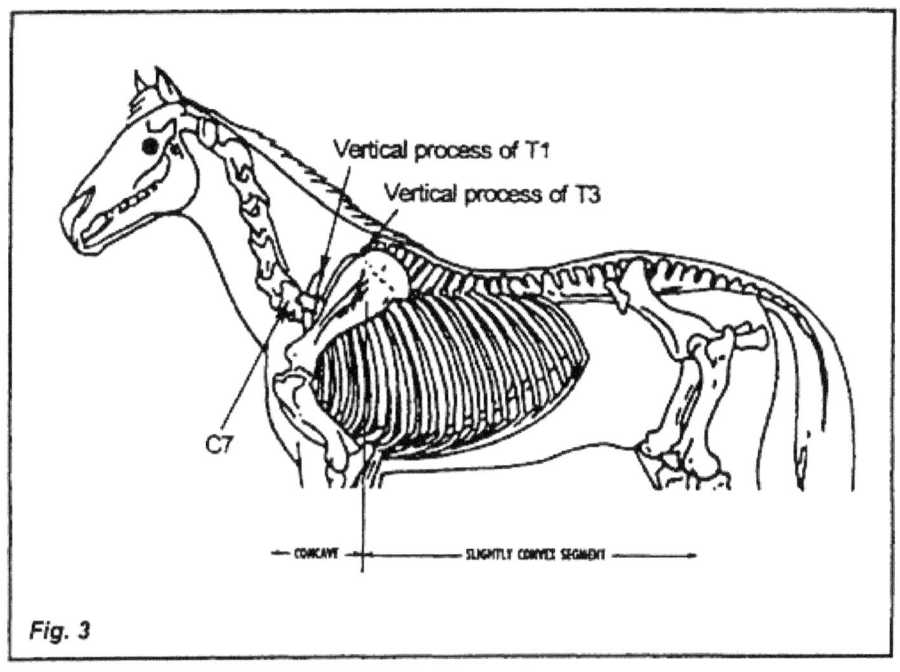

Fig. 3

What are we then going to replace the inside leg with, in order to bend a horse? With our weight! If this latter is displaced inwards with respect to the desired bending, the rib cage is very likely to rotate *outwards,* in order to bring the burden back on a vertical diameter (so as to even up the load borne by each lateral). This rotation, in turn, is the key element of a true bending, as we have seen.

Let's now proceed forward along the horse's spinal column, as we bend it. A horse has 18 thoracic vertebrae. Unlike the cervical vertebrae, which are ahead of the thoracic segment, *these vertebrae cannot "twist."* Now, it happens that this thoracic segment is not uniformly bent in its profile; it is slightly convex from T18 to T4 (the foremost vertebra of the withers we can feel the spine of), and it is concave from T3 to T1 (this concavity propagates to C7, the last cervical vertebra, up to the joint C7-C6) (Fig. 3).

Due to the quasi-impossibility of these thoracic vertebrae "twisting," if the spines of the vertebrae from T18 to T4 rotate left, for instance, the spines of the vertebrae from T3 to T1 will also tend to rotate left. This left rotation will create a lateral bending of the vertebral column right, from T18 to T4, which is a convex segment, and a lateral bending left from T4 to T1, which is a concave segment (Fig. 4).

Therefore, a horse is never *uniformly* bent in one direction; there always is a small part of his vertebral column, right between the shoulders or slightly ahead of them, which more or less bends the other way. ***This is an extremely important discovery.***

This phenomenon is not visible from horseback since the last vertebra we can see the tip of is the fourth thoracic; the segment it is about (T3, T2, T1, C7) lies ahead of it, dipping deeper and deeper down into the horse's neck.

As a matter of fact, when a horse is bent, the reversal of curvature of his spine at the level C7-T1-T2-T3 which appears in a profile view (vertical plane) is translated by a reversal of bend at the same level in the view from above (horizontal plane). The amplitude of this reversal is difficult to evaluate, due to the restricted range of motion of T1 and T2. Still, it does matter through its very existence.

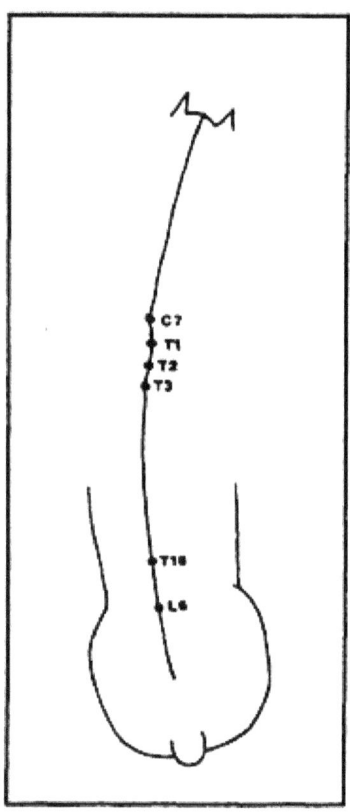

Fig. 4 - Horse bent to the right. The segment C7 - T3 displays reversed bending.

Let's now concentrate on the shoulders. By rotating the rib cage, the bending pushes the sternum inwards. This will, in turn, push the inside shoulder off, entailing (and this will come as a surprise for some) a *forward* movement for this shoulder, a gesture induced by the "tapering" shape of the rib cage at this level and facilitated by the absence of a collar bone in the horse. As a matter of fact, and albeit there is no direct connection between these two anatomical parts, all happens *as if* the shoulders wanted to adapt their position to the locally reversed bending of the spine.

This forward movement of the inside shoulder explains why a horse bent to the right canters easily on the right lead, why moving laterally to the left is much easier when bent to the right (right shoulder-in) than when bent to the left (half-pass to the left).

We now have to examine what would happen if we could bend a horse *uniformly* from head to tail, that is, if this small segment from C7 to T3 were obliged to bend in the same direction as the rest of the spinal column. Bending to the right, for instance, would provoke a rotation to the right of this segment (which is concave), although it induces a rotation to the left of the rest of the spines, back from T4 (which is convex). What do you think would happen at the junction between these two opposite rotations, *all the more as the thoracic vertebrae cannot twist?* A big clash! An immediate blocking of one or more of these first thoracic vertebrae, with as a result a total impossibility for the horse to raise his withers anymore, hence to collect freely and painlessly, if at all (Fig. 5). (Notwithstanding the eventual organic sequels, emphysema for instance, to mention only one, since T1 is so much linked to the para-sympathetic system.)

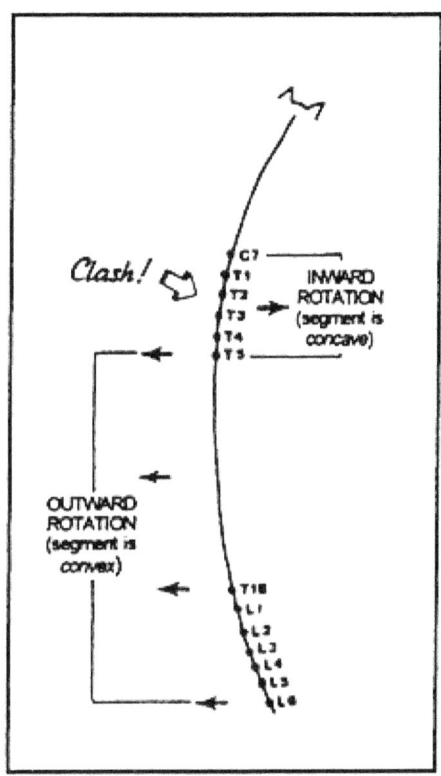

Fig. 5 - What happens when the vertebral column is uniformly bent.

You will tell me that a horse is not fool enough to allow himself to be submitted to such a constraint/that he will by all means try to evade it. Well, I am not so sure.

Let's take, for instance, the half-pass. Difficult to believe at first that such a "classical" movement could have some flaw. Still, it is well known that in a half-pass, the outside shoulder should pass in front of the inside.

There is visibly a contradiction between this requirement, which tends to rotate the rib cage *inwards,* and the inside bending of the whole horse, which tends to rotate the same rib cage *outward. So* there will be a "torque," which will have to be assumed at some level, possibly T1-T2, given the susceptibility of this area.

To prevent this from happening, it is likely that the intelligent horse will give up on being bent altogether, from T4 back to the last lumbar. He will show lateral bending only with his neck, which is supple enough to bend independently from the rest of the body, and collection will be lost to boot. The interest of such a movement, I fail to see.

We should, therefore, perform our half-passes with a *moderate* lateral bending of the horse and a *moderate* crossing over of the front legs, in order to lessen the possibilities of "torque" at whichever level. Too bad for the spectacle, but all the better indeed for the vertebral integrity of the horse.

The threat on this weak C7-T1-T2-T3 segment is, in my opinion, more present in the "haunches-in," a movement, however, supposed to be only introductory to the half-pass, because in this movement the shoulders *have to* (it is an academic requirement) remain perpendicular to the direction of march, involving a strong rotation of the line of shoulders. (Fortunately, most horses don't care and just don't do it!)

And now, I have to quit before the FEI burns me at the stake.

Appendix by Jean-Claude Racinet

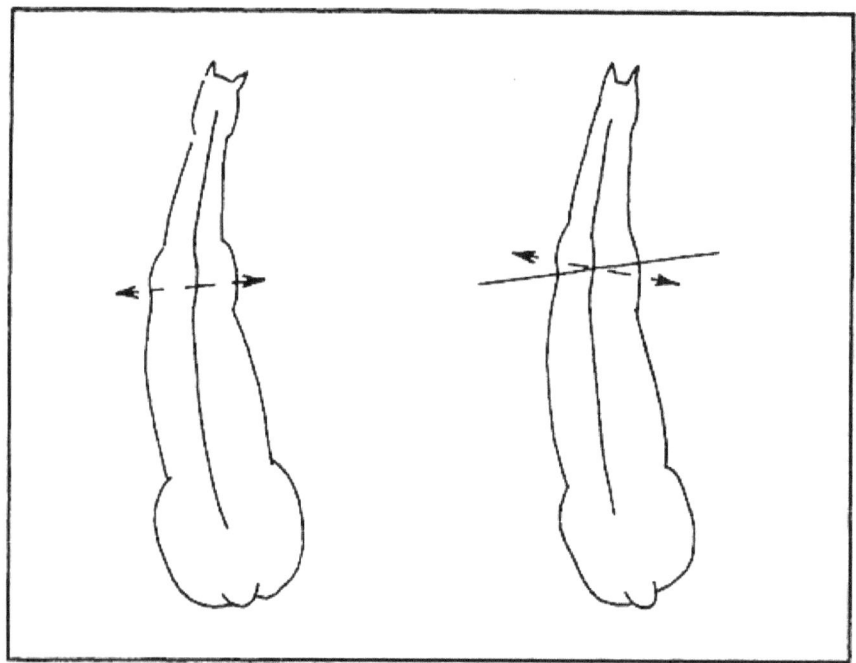

Fig. 6a - Line of shoulders on the circle and shoulder-in conform to local (reversed) bending.

Fig. 6b - Line of shoulders in half-pass, negating the local (reversed) bending.

Epilogue

Twenty years of dialogue with horses

As we enter the third millennium, I am always interested in what my daily encounters with horses will bring me and allow me to understand. The road is long on this path of new knowledge, but it is beautiful and exciting.

In 1986, I announced the inevitable development of this form of medicine to the equine world. We are gaining new evidence of its relevance on a daily basis. I do not pretend to be the creator of equine osteopathy; I merely had the chance to be the first to develop a method. It was time for this to happen; as with any new approach, it was necessary that it had to begin with someone. I say that I had the luck to be that person. My only voluntary action may have been to be daring enough to throw myself at seizing this opportunity when it was presented to me.

Now, around the world, more and more horses from all disciplines are followed by osteopaths who passionately forge ahead into this promising territory.

It is widely understood that osteopathy does not negate the value of conventional veterinary medicine; it adds tools to those who want to help the horse to be more efficient and especially to feel good in their daily work or even simply in their own lives.

The period when conventional veterinarians showed some aggression towards the novelty of osteopathy that they did not comprehend has passed. This was a normal and predictable reaction from them, since veterinary studies do not prepare students at all for the type of reasoning used by osteopaths. Only idiots do not evolve, and there will always be some.

But in life, not everything is black or white, and many veterinarians who have evolved in the right direction may have valid reasons to become aggressive again. I share their concerns. We are now at a stage where the customer must sort through the osteopaths. In fact, demand is such that some people pretend to be osteopaths (without any training) and abuse the credulity of horse owners. These false osteopaths are nevertheless sometimes sincere, but they believe they are competent because they achieved some results by copying stereotypical gestures.

I even think I have a share of responsibility in this regard; no one would dare to bend the spine of a horse before seeing that it was possible! The fact is that it can sometimes seem deceptively simple, but when I unlock a back problem on a horse within a few minutes, the truth is, that it really took me 20 years of study and not just those few minutes that make it seem easy. My surgery professor at the veterinary school used to tell us:

"You'll finally be a good surgeon on the day, when seeing you operate on his horse, your client says: 'It's so easy that I have should have done it myself, rather than paying for it!'"

Osteopathy is a medicine that can be learned. Not only does it require years of study, but it must also be joined by real knowledge of classic pathology.

First, I will suggest some criteria to use to allow an initial screening for selecting an osteopath that is intended to give you the basics not to call back those who are not actually osteopaths in the sense I mean:

A non-osteopath:

He who comes from canvassing and offers his/her services. This applies to any profession; the good practitioners are well-known by word of mouth and are already widely sought out.

He who first asks for all symptoms and disorders that are present in the horse. This means that he will decide what he will do by reasoning from what has been said of the horse, and not by "asking" the horse what its imbalances are. It may be that he/she knows techniques but he/she is not trained in palpation and the "manual listening." I recall here that a true osteopath does not address symptoms; he/she looks for imbalances in the patient that he proposes to resolve.

Whoever administers a sedative before handling the horse. Not only does he/she want to impose his/her views and actions onto the animal and he/she also may be trying to avoid kicks, but it is actually more dangerous to practice osteopathy when the patient is sedated; the nervous system does not record information, changes in tension and rebalancing resulting from the manipulations. Moreover, it proves that the practitioner's method is not based on information gained from the organism that is being treated and therefore cannot know exactly at what time to act.

Manipulation itself is a dialogue with the body of another being and must therefore depend on full awareness with all reflexes participating in the dialogue.

Finally, a horse under sedation doesn't have the same preservation reflexes that would otherwise warn and prevent the therapist from going too far.

Anyone who is aggressive and fights the horse to impose on him.

Or he/she is obviously intimidated by the horse and wants absolutely to get his/her way at the cost of conflict. You cannot bring any good to a patient if you intend to hurt! That said, if an owner calls back a therapist who has already shown aggression once to his horse, it shows how little he/she cares about the welfare of his/her companion [horse]; i.e. above all else it's showing that the owner wants results for himself/herself and his/her equestrian success, his/her horse is barely a means or a tool get to his/her personal goals. Such riders can simply continue with fake therapists; a true osteopath would not want to have any part of this.

Those who decide in advance how many times he/she will see the animal. A real osteopath proposes to a patient to help him find a new equilibrium and therefore we do not know how long it will take to be put "back on its feet." It may be that we need a next intervention but we need to give the client sufficient criteria so he/she can appreciate the timing and conditions necessary for another treatment with additional progress.

Those who use restraints. This includes everything from the twitch to the use of ropes to restrain limbs. This practitioner feels nothing, beside the deserved kicks and the ones he's/she's trying to avoid. When a horse is opposed to manipulation, it is often because he has a good reason to be against it; more likely it is because the proposed manipulation is not the right one for him. We'll talk more about this notion of gesture that the animal instinctively expects.

Whoever sends systematically a debt collector to those who do not pay quickly. (Yes, there are some who do it systematically!) This may be a joke but it is valid for any care taker, osteopath or veterinarian. Aside from the case of notorious bad payers you need to avoid or square them off, the first question to ask when facing nonpayment is to find out why the customer is not satisfied. The happy customers pay! This is not the care taker to tell the client that it is a good therapist, it is the customer to confirm it.... and it's in paying that customers say they felt a real intention of giving good care, even if the result cannot be guaranteed.

Whoever denigrates previously given care, especially one that systematically denigrated conventional medicine. A true osteopath is not the superman who holds the only truth; this is a man who uses other forms of reasoning to heal but also understands the interest in treatment he does not use.

Those who accuse systematically the customer or another therapist to be responsible for the problem. This behavior also exists in other forms of medicine. It is a way to avoid responsibility by saying: "I'll do what I can, but you must not blame me, it's because of what has been done before." The problem is not there, the client requests that his animal gets better, he is not asking who caused the animal not to be well. Moreover, when we chooe to heal, we must take control of the case and the responsibilities that follow from them. Faced with a severe case, the client calls above all not to be responsible for the death of the animal. We must actually assume the responsibilities and worries, free the customer of this hardship.

The one who adds an anti-inflammatory injection or infiltration with his manipulations. This is intended for both veterinary and non-veterinary osteopaths asking the customer to make such a treatment as soon as possible. Not only does this mean they have some doubts about their own effectiveness and want a spectacular result, but mostly it is never done because it's very harmful in the follow ups. Indeed, these drugs disconnect all information from the body to the nervous system. In such a case, the horse does not have the notion of the changes in tension and balance of the skeleton and muscles. Having "in mind" the old scheme of his body, it will make movements that do not correspond to its new equilibrium and it will soon be anarchy. That is why in this case the results are often very bad and the horse ends up with blocks that have nothing to do with the problems we wanted to treat. The animal quickly becomes a very good customer who always has a new disorder to treat! I have nothing against infiltration well done when it is necessary to repair damaged tissues, but it is imperative to wait eight to ten days after the manipulation to administer this kind of products.

And we could go on like this for a long time, but we must understand that we are in a period of anarchy and everything can be done, and even the opposite, under this term of osteopathy. Sorting will be done anyhow in time...

I would now like to return to what horses told me and explained about them and caring for each other.

* * *

In this journey with horses, what I have retained to be the most important for now is the fact that good health is a personal concept.

Good health is fortunately not to have anything wrong with us, but it is to agree with all the quirks and anomalies we do have.

"Anomalies" is the adequate term. An anomaly is what comes out of the norm. This leads me to talk about medical examination processes, new imaging material and of insurance or pre-purchase exams. Medicine has established statistical standards of good health. It is effectively statistics; the urea in the blood, the shape of a bone, echo-graphic image of a tendon, etc. are averages of evaluation established after examining a large number of horses. Therefore these are criteria to respect and to which we must stay closer statistically when treating a large population of horses. But we forget that while no horse is the norm, yet we try to apply it to the individual. We forget that there is no statistics in a population reduced to a single unit!

A horse that's going well is a horse who found its balance. Healing a horse is not making him an average horse (in the statistical sense) but it is to make him feel good even if he seems odd to us.

Many examples come to mind. For instance, when the *aplombs*[16] are finally normal after several trimming and shoeing sessions to get the horses ready for a breed shows, their movement has paradoxically regressed.

I'm not suggesting we leave all horses on bad *aplombs*; we must modify all *aplombs* leading to locomotion disorders. The pathology of the *aplombs* is not an aesthetic issue; instead it is pathological if it results in a problem

---

16   *aplombs*: describes legs and feet conformation when the horse is standing still.

in the horse's movement. Again, it is a recurring theme that you should listen to the horse, and carefully watch his movement instead of listening to the opinions of persons based on measurements and statistical findings alone.

In this particular case of the manner in which a horse stands, the search for a standard to satisfy judges at a breed show is even more ridiculous. Trimming and compensation does not affect the genes and will therefore not transmit to the offspring! But I think the competition breed shows are made to preserve the criteria of race....

New examination processes, such as scintigraphy, ultrasonography, MRI, thermography, etc. are actually in progress and should not be neglected, but admit that we have not yet mastered their interpretation. We now find abnormalities that would never be suspected previously, and there are so many things that we cannot conclude on the state of health of the animal. Often the practitioner himself is panicked by everything he finds wrong with the horse and sometimes does not dare to take a decision which commits his responsibility, as in the case of a purchase exam. This is simply because he is losing the habit of palpating and feeling.

When will we understand that these exams are only allowing us to search for the normal horse, which fortunately does not exist, and meets statistical standards?

These exam processes, just as the radiograph, should be used to check if what we found is true or not. A lesion that is not accompanied by disorders is just an anomaly, not a disease. It may become one; any living individual can become ill even if we did not find any anomalies with the actual process.

Osteopathy and its manual listening, as well as the acupuncture with "trigger points," often allow us to discover if there is an underlying disorder. With a copy of the report enumerating all the anomalies of a horse, one can often interpret which items pose problems for the organism and this suggests even how to prepare for competition accordingly. It is indeed then the body speaking, and not a machine confirming what man thinks the organism should be.

And most importantly, what interest would there be to find a horse without anomalies? This would mean that it is in the standard and nobody seems to even notice that a champion is by definition an abnormal!

It is not normal to be stronger, faster, stronger or more skillful than others! Looking for a champion therefore is looking for an abnormal! Suppose he could have other anomalies and we need to able to sort through these anomalies.

How is it that some racehorses with multiple wins with an abnormal frames are still always ahead? The day has not yet arrived when a machine will distinguish good defects from bad defects. Human interpretation will still be required for a long time to make conclusions, with the wealth of information, instinctive feelings and always the risk of errors that may occur. Infallibility does not exist but human appreciation will always be more highly valued than the statistical conclusions of a machine which is obeyed and we dare not to contradict. We will never evade our responsibilities by hiding behind stupid, peremptory opinions incapable of the slightest nuances of a machine. Those who will never assert their intuition to the findings of a machine do group medicine, which may be useful for a large group, but we should be wary when they speak of an individual.

It is true that many champions are not insurable according to the criteria of insurance companies, but where is the problem?

Should we refuse a horse because of a risk which has not been proven when we know that any horse, even healthy, can die of colic overnight? Then let's add clauses to the contract to protect the insurer (a shame!). But let us take the risk of a great career for the pleasure we will receive. And let us be humble enough to admit that intuition may presents flaws.

To show how osteopathy can bring healing to serious problems, I will cite the case of a racing mare I had to treat in England. This is a three year old filly who won a big group race at the end of May, a few years ago. I was called early in July because she showed intolerable back pain and could no longer even bear the weight of her jockey. Her program included for her to run another big race in August before leaving for the stud farm. When the veterinarian in charge of her care (skilled man whom I have a lot of respect for) learned that I was coming to see the filly, he came and picked me up at the airport and first took me over tos his clinic to review radiographs and the different exams he had performed. He showed me a catastrophic file with arthritis, welded vertebras with bone proliferation and obvious inflamed areas. He was trying to tell me that at this stage it was useless to try anything. I immediately reassured him that I had no intention or pretention in giving the filly a normal spine back. I just added that in some way, six weeks ago, this filly had the same spine, ran without pain and won the race. I would therefore simply try to propose to her to find back her equilibrium maybe odd but painless she had at the time of her victory.

I manipulated what I thought was in acute conflict and what the palpation allowed me to detect. It is not radiography or scintigraphy of the spine that told me what to do but uniquely the palpation. It is the entire body of the filly who guided me in the motions to do.

Six weeks later, she came in second in the race. Mission accomplished, she then went to a large stud farm to contribute to her breed.

I did not modify her vertebras or spine. I had the chance to find out how she could get along with her abnormal spine she had for a long time which did not stop her to perform as long as she had the false equilibrium that suited this oddity.

* * *

Nobody "repaired" a damaged bone (aside in the case of a fracture but it's the organism that repairs, the surgeon is ensuring that the repair is done in a correct position).

In the case of lameness, decalcification or navicular disease, achieving healing means that the bone is no longer inflamed and the treatment, whatever it is, orthopedic or medicated, allowed the horse to get back to its initial state before the lameness.

It's worth it to spend a little time on lameness: The nerve transmitting pain in an organism is a specific fiber which is its only role. They have non negligible particularity, the pain impulses they transmit are controlled by a threshold response. As long as the pain transmission has not reached a certain threshold, it can't reach the brain due to a barricade. In a movement like a misstep, a change in the *aplomb* will let the pain message pass the threshold and reach the brain. The threshold collapses and lameness sets in and the local lesion is not serious anymore. The brain then being aware of the problem immediately sends orders to circulation changes, edema, etc.... These orders are unfortunately often exaggerated and worsen the situation. Healing is to restore the original threshold response. It is obtained by calming inflammation (provided the horse is at complete rest), or by changing the *aplomb* to find a position that calms the crisis and allows the nervous system to raise the threshold, using manipulation to allow the organism to find a more adequate balance.

We then understand that a limping horse has always had exactly the same abnormal bone before and during his lameness, and when it is "cured" this bone is still abnormal but the horse no longer knows. The threshold response of the concerned nerve fibers is simply reinstalled between the lesion and the nervous system.

Therefore, I dare say that if a horse does not know he has a good reason to limp, it is important not to tell him!

I want to talk more precisely about flexion tests now widely abused. It seems that we are moving towards a medicine or "palpate and feel" which becomes more and more "make suffer and watch." That such a practice test on a lame member can see if we increase lameness, this is very useful. But causing pain on a healthy horse and taking the risk of putting the nervous system on alert from a lesion that it did not know is, in my opinion, an error of which we must be wary.

I remember a race horse who had won everything at two years old, without limping, but we knew he had fragments of cartilage in both knees. When he won one of the biggest American races at the end of two years, his owner decided to take advantage of his visit to the United States to get his knee surgery done. The operation went flawlessly, I saw the radiographs done afterward and the knees were at last perfect, without any aberrant bone reaction. But he went back to work as a horse that has bad knees and has never run properly since!

At two years, he did not know he had abnormal knees, but we told him by operating when there was no justification…. This may be the surgery itself that passed information to a correct threshold that was always used, it may be because the knees had other anomalies that current techniques do not yet know how to detect, we can imagine everything, but the fact is there. We should only intervene or cause pain when the patient shows symptoms and that he "knows" that he has a problem.

We should treat or operate on those who suffer, but we must respect the personal balance of those who are well. It will be time to act in case of problems.

I write throughout this book you need to know how to ask the patient, to listen to him. That's what it's all about. The body not only knows the problems it has, but it often has an instinctive sense of what it would need to feel better. In case of neck pain in a human, a person tries to relieve it by turning his/her head. One feels instinctively movement should be done to liberate its own cervical vertebrae. Without any concept of anatomy, we look precisely for the gesture that would make a good osteopath, but it requires the intervention of the other: the nervous system that has installed a spasm as a precaution will not dare go beyond that spasm. Significant detail, it is not this movement to avoid pain; it is a painful movement because we feel that at the end of that movement relief will be there.

This is exactly the same with a horse. The osteopath should know to feel the movement that the animal expects instinctively. When he takes the horse's foot, he does not know yet the precise direction he will take with the limb. It is a very fine and short dialogue, but precise, which is established between the two individuals. The therapist does not impose anything, he follows and accompanies the movement evoked by the horse, until a stage where the horse hesitates and pulls on his member to evade the position reached. It is at this precise moment that the spasm gives and manipulation is done thanks to the combined action of the two protagonists. It is the team man-horse who finds the movement, and in this short time, the exchange is not only mechanical, it's not a question to hurt or not; if the movement following this dialogue is correct, the horse will participate even if it is uncomfortable or hurt him. If the movement is wrong, the horse opposes: it can run away or paw even if it does not hurt him. Even if everything goes by feel, it is essential to have in mind a perfect mental picture of the anatomy, the blockage and what we want to achieve.

Note in passing that I said the horse pulled on his limb. I say this to all those who pull like crazy on the limbs and joints of the animal. When it is the horse that pulls his own, at the right time and in the right direction, the osteopath does not pull, he gently holds on at the precise moment the horse made the decision. Similarly for the neck it is to support the movement and resist briefly when the horse suddenly brings back his head. Resistance to apply depends on the case and especially the horse, but it is never "bend" the neck. Thus, if there are a lot of techniques to know, it is to understand what is happening and be able to leave the basis in favor of a dialogue that is new every time.

Do not worry, osteopathy is not a panacea, it is an approach to health that suits me better, and I wish to all the therapists of all methods to feel much in agreement with themselves in what they do. In all disciplines there will always be people whose motivations are not as sincere and beautiful as they should be, but it is also the responsibility of the customer to sort out and do not promote the development of more or less suspicious behavior which does not honor anyone.

* * *

I mentioned in this book that the horses have actually told me. We hear a lot about the current wave of "horse-whisperers," those who "whisper" things to horses and everyone gets involved. There would be many pages to write about that.

Know that the true horse whisperers such as Monty Roberts and some others are people who have not learned how to talk to horses; they have first listened to allow them to speak a language horses already knew.In the relationship that osteopathy has allowed me to establish with the horses, I'm not at the stage to talk to them or even to whisper to them anything, I want to *listen* in order to seek to bring them the help they need from what their body expresses to me.

If we listen, horses have a lot more to bring us than we can give them. They kept their instinct, which is a body language infinitely varied and precise. We, poor humans, have completely forsaken our instinct because of the pride to have discovered and created a talking language. The human language is a great thing, but it has amputated a lot of nuances that we have not retained. We humbly relearn a lot from animals, and it is best to listen.

The osteopathy is neither a technique nor a belief. Those who teach and those who learn gestures without the feeling (in the sense of feeling that must accompany them) are not and will never be osteopaths. It is of course the same with classic medicine...

When holding a horse in my arms to manipulate and to try to help him, I do not whisper anything; I try to be available for quiet listening. He talks about him but also me and us.

I try to be the man who listens to horses.

About this Author

Born in November 1944 in France, Dr. Dominique Giniaux started his career as a "mainstream" veterinarian in 1968 and went on treating horses in a "classical" manner until 1981. Although very respectful of and adept at this established knowledge, he later turned to "holistic" medicines, like acupuncture and osteopathy, which he studied first on humans.

Dr. Giniaux was the first in the world to practice structural osteopathy with the equine. His fame soon became international when he was called to lecture outside of France and in the United States for the IVAS (International Veterinary Acupuncture Society).

About this book

The lay public is probably less familiar with the concept of osteopathy than the concept of chiropractics. Let it be stated that both acknowledge the pathological effect of vertebral lesions (subluxations) upon the functioning of the nervous system. Osteopathy, however, may practice a different type of manipulation. It concerns itself with the whole structure—that is to say, vertebrae, but also all other joints, muscles, ligaments, and fascia. Osteopathy holds that if the structure is blocked in one of its components, health will be jeopardized, since the flux of energy which pervades the organism will be impaired. It is a "manual" medicine, where the healer (physician, veterinarian) is "listening" to his/her patient. Hence the title of this book, "What the Horses Have Told Me."

Enthusiastic, curious, and brilliant, Dr. Giniaux is a researcher who passionately tries to understand, not only with his brain but also with his heart and senses, the exhilarating phenomenon called "life."

www.ingramcontent.com/pod-product-compliance
Lightning Source LLC
Chambersburg PA
CBHW052026290426
44112CB00014B/2398